# WILD
# BRITAIN
# WILD
# IRELAND

Unique National Parks, Nature Reserves and Biosphere Reserves

# WILD BRITAIN, WILD IRELAND

Previous double page: Loch Lomond and the Trossachs is Scotland's first national park and boasts an idyllic landscape of lakes, rivers, forests and villages nestling among rolling hills.

Bottom: Aira Force is a waterfall in England's Lake District National Park, which tumbles 20 metres / 66 feet down into Lake Ullswater not far from the mouth of Aira Beck. A beautiful natural spectacle and therefore also a popular destination for day trips.

The Isle of Thanet is an island in the south-east of England that was originally completely separate from the mainland. It was only joined later with the building of several bridges. Botany Bay creates a popular beach backdrop.

Walkers taking any of the numerous hiking trails through the Gap of Dunloe are surrounded by unique natural landscapes. The gorge lies in County Kerry in the Republic of Ireland, at the island's south-western tip.

Over millions of years, rugged volcanic and lava rocks have formed this strange rock landscape on the beach of Kilfarassy, on Ireland's Copper Coast. The atmosphere changes with each passing hour and season.

The Isle of Skye lies in Scotland's Inner Hebrides and serves as dramatic and impressive testimony to the wild beauty of the landscapes of Western Europe.

# ABOUT THIS BOOK

Scarcely anywhere else is nature as rich and abundant as it is on this north-western archipelago. The wild beauties of the British Isles are landscapes full of mystery and legend, full of tragedy and fortune, that once inspired hosts of poets and have lost none of their poetic majesty since. Ireland, Scotland, England and Wales – each region has its own characteristic features, with all of them sharing a landscape shaped by wind and weather and featuring seemingly endless fields and meadows, picturesque river courses, mysterious forests and steep cliffs tumbling down into the sea.

**The rugged peaks of the Cuillin Hills, the highest on the Scottish Isle of Skye, are almost completely barren. Further down there are shrubs, ice-blue mountain lakes and wild streams.**

# CONTENTS

Some of the most striking rock formations in the spectacular natural phenomenon of Giant's Causeway in Northern Ireland have even been given vivid names such as "the Giant's Boot", "the Camel's Hump" and "the Wishing Chair".

# THE BRITISH ISLES

Short summer nights, dark winter months - the northern part of the British Isles is a little bit like the Arctic. But the Gulf Stream means there's no permafrost. Instead, there's a truly extraordinary light; especially in summer, when sunrise seems to follow just after sunset. That is when mysterious rock formations cast long shadows, and mosses and grasses glimmer intensely in that strange light. The landscapes of the British Isles vary widely but there is one thing they certainly have in common: the green. It seems to come in thousands of shades here and coats the crags and plateaus like a deep, velvety carpet.

**To the west of York, between the Lake District and the North York Moors, is the hiking paradise that is the Yorkshire Dales. A beautiful 18.5 kilometre / 11 mile circular trail leads along the White Scars from Ingleton to Chapel-le-Dale.**

# DUBLIN BAY
## UNESCO Biosphere Reserve

In 1981, UNESCO recognised the significance of Dublin Bay, with its rare and internationally important habitats and wildlife species of wildlife, and designated it a Biosphere Reserve. To support sustainable development, UNESCO's concept of a Biosphere has evolved to include not just areas of ecological value but also the areas surrounding them. Thus, since 2015, the reserve has been expanded to include everything that reflects its economic, cultural and tourism importance. It now covers an area of 300 square kilometres / 116 square miles. Nowadays over 300,000 people live within the newly enlarged Biosphere reserve, which is divided into three zones. The core zone has areas of high natural value, the buffer zone has public and private green spaces such as parks and golf-courses, and the transition zone has harbours, ports, and residential and industrial areas.

## At a glance

**Location:** Dublin Bay, a delta-shaped estuary of the rivers Liffey and Dodder, opening into the Irish Sea on the east coast of Ireland near Dublin
**Area:** 300 km² /116 mi²
**Designation as UNESCO Biosphere Reserve:** 1981
**www.dublinbaybiosphere.ie**

The former fishing village of Howth is now one of the most popular day trip destinations in the bay. Just before the lighthouse there is a path taking you up the hill to Howth summit, from which point you can feast your eyes on the whole expanse of Dublin Bay.

Although there is sometimes a strong breeze blowing, you can savour the picturesque sunset with this stunning panoramic view of the sea. If you're lucky you can catch a glimpse of a large freight ship or cruise liner.

# WICKLOW MOUNTAINS
## National Park

Founded in 1991, the Wicklow Mountains National Park covers a nature conservation area of about 200 square kilometres / 77 square miles close to the east coast of Ireland. This mountain landscape of volcanic origin is made up of granite and schists rounded by Ice Age glaciers. Deeply rutted by rushing streams, areas of bog and heathland, broadleaf and coniferous woodland alternate across the hillsides. The highest elevation is Lugnaquilla at 925 metres / 3,035 feet, with the source of the river Slaney at its southwesterly base. On a clear day you can see all the way to the Irish Sea from its summit. The Wicklow Mountains were the setting for a gold rush in 1795, but the excitement didn't last long. The mine was exhausted after just a few years and a mere 300 kg / 661 lb had been found. Nowadays, it is no longer gold hunters who are attracted to the area but those searching for peace and relaxation.

## At a glance

**Location:** mountain range in the east and southeast of Ireland, running in a north-south direction, directly from South Dublin to the counties of Wicklow and Wexford
**Area:** 200 km² / 77 mi²
**Foundation:** 1991
**www.wicklowmountainsnational park.ie**

Brightly coloured hills covered in swathes of grasses and heathers (top picture) are typical of this boggy landscape. It is hard to believe that this pure, natural idyll is only one hour from the vibrant city of Dublin.

Around 130 kilometres / 80 miles long, the Wicklow Way is a long-distance trail which runs from the suburbs of Dublin across the mountains. The remains of old native woodland are now only to be found near the rivers (left); the small coniferous forests are plantations used for timber production.

# COPPER COAST
## UNESCO Global Geopark

The Copper Coast Geopark is a designated area comprising a stretch of the southern coast of Ireland in County Waterford, extending for some 17 kilometres / 10 miles from Kilfarrasy in the east to Stradbally in the west. Both the coast and the geopark are named after the historic 19th century copper-mining industry, whose legacies now form a tourist attraction. A local interest group formed in 1997 came up with the idea of the geopark.

The area, with its spectacular cliffs, was declared a European Geopark in 2001 and a UNESCO Global Geopark in 2004. This geologically diverse area contains records of Palaeozoic volcanism and the last ice age - a heritage which comes to life for the visitor. One example is the visitor centre at Monksland Church in Knockmahon, which is dedicated to the Geopark and its 460 million year old history.

## At a glance

**Location:** in County Waterford, from Kilfarrasy to Stradbally
**Area:** 50 km² / 19 mi²
**Foundation:** 1997
**Designation as UNESCO Global Geopark:** 2004
**www.coppercoastgeopark.com**

The Gaulstown Dolmen is a historical attraction consisting of six upright stones which form a chamber with a five metre / sixteen feet-long cap stone. The portal stones protrude from the ground and are approximately two metres / six feet high.

The small cove of Goat Island Beach is situated around five kilometres / three miles to the west of Ardmore in County Waterford. The remote beach faces south and is difficult to find, which is why it is considered a local treasure.

# KERRY
## UNESCO Biosphere Reserve

# KERRY
## UNESCO Biosphere Reserve

The Killarney Biosphere Reserve was founded in 1982 within the Killarney National Park. The UNESCO International Coordination Committee confirmed the application in 2017, although it identified the need for certain actions. According to their report, the buffer and transition zones needed to be expanded. This meant that the Biosphere had to be renamed, thus the reserve has been known as the Kerry Biosphere Reserve since

2018. The core zone area covers 10,260 hectares / 25,353 acres, which corresponds to the area of Killarney National Park. The buffer zone is 531 hectares / 1,312 acres in size and is between the National Park and Killarney town. The transition zone is 54,210 hectares / 133,955 acres. It will be exciting to see how the reserve will change over time. Regardless of what happens, the place contains fascinating sites of natural beauty including one of the oldest remaining oak forests.

**The reserve on the Killarney National Park is in the southwest, very close to Killarney, "the most popular town in Ireland". After Dublin, it is the most visited tourist destination in Ireland.**

## At a glance

**Location:** between Killarney National Park and Killarney town
**Area:** 102 km² / 39 mi²
**Designation as UNESCO Biosphere Reserve:** 1982

The Kerry Biosphere Reserve in the Killarney National Park is very close to the Ring of Kerry– a picturesque, 179 kilometre / 111 mile-long panoramic coast road winding through the heart of County Kerry.

## Sessile oaks

This broad-leafed deciduous tree grows up to 30 metres / 100 feet high and can reach an age of between 800 and 1,000 years. It has a loose, spreading crown with even foliage of deep-green, glossy, leathery leaves which are somewhat lighter on the underside and covered in silky hairs. The tree is in bloom between April and May and bears large, pointed brown buds at the tips of the twigs. The fruits - acorns - can be seen from September. The sessile oak is named after these, because several acorns grow in a cluster without stalks (sessile). Although acorns are inedible for humans because of their tannins, they are a valuable source of food for animals.

## European hollies

Hollies (Ilex) are evergreen or deciduous trees. They typically have leathery, dark-green leaves, often serrated with thorny teeth, and their fruit (drupes) are usually bright red. In Ireland, they have long been traditionally associated with Christmas. However, both the leaves and fruit are very poisonous. The dense greenish wood of the Ilex was once very popular for inlay work in furniture. Nowadays, it is mostly used for making walking sticks.

## Common yew

There are two kinds of common yew trees, those with female and those with male flowers. The male flowers are yellowish in colour. Each female flower has just a single ovule, surrounded by sterile bracts. After pollination, a poisonous false fruit is produced. It has a fleshy, bright-red skin with mucilaginous fruit flesh forming a cup-like surround for the actual fruit containing the seed. Yew timber is hard and elastic, hence it used to be very popular with archers.

# KILLARNEY
## National Park

"I hope that Muckross will be made a real garden of friendship, and that it will be the greatest playground in the world" - this is how Arthur Rose Vincent expressed himself in the endowment document with which he presented the villa to the Irish state. Built in 1932, it is situated on a small peninsula between two lakes, Muckross Lake and Lough Leane. Designed in the Victorian style by Scottish architect William Burn, the original construction of

the manor house for the Herbert family was carried out between 1838 and 1843. Today, Muckross House has been converted into a museum and with its luxuriant gardens it is the centrepiece of the Killarney National Park. In 2000, the Traditional Farms museum was added to the facility. The National Park site also contains the remains of Muckross Abbey, a Franciscan monastery which acquired its current appearance in the 15th century.

**Numerous interesting areas of bog and heath can be found in the high plateau of the park. Rare varieties of moss and lichen grow on the tree trunks with particular abundance thanks to the mild climate caused by the nearby Atlantic.**

## At a glance

**Location:** in County Kerry on the Iveragh peninsula in the southwest of the Republic of Ireland
**Area:** 100 km² / 38 mi²
**Foundation:** 1932
www.killarneynationalpark.ie

The gardens of the manor house are surrounded by lakes with stone bridges dating from the 16th century. A one-hour walk takes you from Muckross to the Torc waterfall (picture centre) to the southeast of Lough Leane.

## Upper Lake

Named after its US American donor, the Bourn Vincent Memorial Park with its three lakes, which makes up about a quarter of the area of the Killarney National Park, was designated as a Biosphere Reserve by UNESCO in 1982 because it provides a unique retreat for native woodland and aquatic animals. The long narrow Upper Lake, where cormorants overwinter, is located in the southern part. Visitors will find the most beautiful vista from Ladies View. This vantage point was given its name in the 19th century because it is said that Queen Victoria's Ladies-in-waiting were enchanted by the overwhelming wonders of nature they witnessed here.

## Torc Mountain

Torc Mountain and the torrential waterfall of the same name are synonymous with Killarney. The easily recognisable shape of Torc mountain can be seen from most parts of the town and the surrounding National Park. The mountain rises from the shores of Muckross Lake over many of the most popular beauty spots in the area. For anyone who grew up in Killarney, a trip to Torc Waterfall was a regular occurrence. Its close proximity to the town and ease of access made it a popular excursion for young and old on a summer's day.

## Purple Mountain

The distinctive combination of mountains, lakes, woods and waterfalls gives the area an exceptionally scenic beauty. Purple Mountain offers an especially breathtaking picture-postcard panorama. Purple Mountain gets its name from the colour of the sandstone rock which emits a purple hue under certain light conditions. Mountain climber love it, although - or maybe because - at 830 metres / 2,723 feet, it is not Ireland's highest peak. The ascent from north to south offers the easiest climb and the best views.

# SKELLIG ISLANDS
## UNESCO World Heritage Site

Top: Blue Man's Rock is a crag lying just a few metres / yards away from the south shore of Great Skellig. Bottom: Grey seals are frequently to be found here as guests resting alongside the multitudinous seabirds.

Around 12 kilometres / seven and a half miles distant from the Irish coast, a barren rock, shrouded in foam, protrudes from the sea. This is Skellig Michael, where one of Ireland's most important archaeological sites is to be found. This monastic site, dedicated to the archangel Michael, was probably founded in the 7th century and, for unknown reasons, abandoned in the 12th century. The walls of the oratories and monks' cells are built into dry-stone, bee-hive-shaped structures in a style which is typical of early Irish architecture. Next to the remains of a 12th century church there is another staircase, which has around 500 steps to enable the pilgrim to climb to the highest peak of the island. The seven hectare / 17 acre neighbouring island of Little Skellig has been a bird sanctuary since 1987 and access to it is forbidden. Among other things, it hosts one of the largest northern gannet populations in the world.

## At a glance

**Location:** about 12 kilometres / 7.5 miles from the coast of Kerry
**Area:** 0.22 km² / 0.085 mi²
**UNESCO World Heritage Site:** since 1996

Their cream-coloured heads, light grey beaks and eyes outlined as though with ink give northern gannets their elegant appearance. Their screeching call, which can be heard from Little Skellig, is somewhat less beautiful, though.

# Northern Gannets
## (Morus bassanus)

The Northern Gannet is a goose-sized seabird. It lives in large colonies in which several thousand breeding pairs raise their young. The preferred breeding grounds of northern gannets are steep crags near the coastline. So it is no wonder that the seven hectare / 17 acre island of Little Skellig, with 27,000 breeding pairs, is one of the largest gannet colonies in the world. Successful pairs incubate one plain, white, goose-sized egg per season. After six

weeks the chick hatches, wrinkly, naked and black as ebony. Within three months it will have changed into a fluffy white puffball. At that time of year, Little Skellig is just one great thronging and bustling. The chicks' plumage has grown out practically pure white, all except for the black wing and tail tips. They are skilful gliders thanks to their narrow wings, which can reach a width of two metres / six feet. Their movements on land may be rather ungainly but they are deft flyers and plunge divers. They dive into the sea like a lightning bolt from great heights. Although northern gannets have few natural enemies, their lives are characterised by a daily struggle against water and weather.

# THE BURREN
## Nationalpark | UNESCO Global Geopark

The Gaelic language word Boireann, from which "Burren" is derived, means "stony place". In the midst of this heather-lined landscape, you keep finding prehistoric remains such as the Poulnabrone Dolmen, which weighs several tonnes (bottom left).

The Ice Age left its distinctive mark on the Burren, which occupies around 250 square kilometres / 96 square miles to the north of Ennis. Retreating glaciers ground down the limestone to a flat, karst landscape riven with furrows, and left behind plant seeds from widely distant regions, from which its very distinctive vegetation results. Since 1991, 15 square kilometres / six square miles of the region have been protected as the Burren National Park. But the Burren

doesn't just attract nature lovers who can hike through a stalactite cave system that stretches over more than a kilometre / more than half a mile in the Ailwee Cave; it also draws archaeology enthusiasts. The main attraction for them is the Poulnabrone Dolmen, a megalithic grave that is around 5,000 years old, in which the bones of 33 humans have been found. Numerous remains of other graves, forts and ritual sites are dispersed throughout the whole Burren area.

**Rare, rock-loving plants bloom in the Burren National Park, including water avens, wild thyme, mountain everlasting, mountain avens, fly orchids and bird's foot trefoil (pictured clockwise from top left).**

## At a glance

**Location:** Burren & Cliffs of Moher Geopark, limestone pavement in the north west of County Clare
**Area:** 530 km² / 204 mi² (15 km² / 5.8 mi² of which is national park)
**Foundation:** 1991
**Designation as UNESCO Global Geopark:** 2015
**www.burrengeopark.ie**

# CLIFFS OF MOHER
## UNESCO Global Geopark

Cliffs rising to over 200 metres / 656 feet high cover the area between Liscannor and Doolin, providing a breathtaking coastal spectacle. Hikers here can explore a beautiful 35 kilometre / 22 mile trail. You can get a real impression of the force of the Atlantic breakers here as you take in the dizzying views from the Cliffs of Moher down to the fiercely crashing sea-spray and the eroding rocky spikes. Unfortunately, the influx of visitors has led to the natural spectacle been unattractively obscured by parking areas, cafés and platforms, especially near O'Brien's Tower, which was built in 1835 as a viewing tower. The southern end of the long stretch of cliffs near the secluded Hag's Head presents an impressive display, especially in the evening when the setting sun lights up the vast layers of sandstone and schist.

## At a glance

**Location:** Burren and Cliffs of Moher Geopark, limestone pavement in the north west of County Clare in Ireland
**Area:** 530 km² / 240 mi²
**Designation as UNESCO Global Geopark:** 2015
**www.cliffsofmoher.ie**

No visit to Ireland is complete without a visit to the Cliffs of Moher. These legendary steep cliffs reach 214 metres / 702 feet at their highest point and are the home of more than 20 varieties of sea bird.

The Cliffs of Moher are the most famous cliffs in Ireland. The name comes from the word Mothar (pronounced "moher"). It refers to a ruin, now overrun with plants, which was once the residence of the chieftains of the province of Munster. Near the cliffs, next to Hag's Head, there is an old ruin called Moher O'Ruan, which ultimately gave the Cliffs of Moher their name.

# CLIFFS OF MOHER
## UNESCO Global Geopark

The cliffs were formed around 320 million years ago. One of the attractions is the viewing tower, built in 1835. If you climb up the winding stairs, you will share an unbelievable view with its many visitors.

# CONNEMARA
## National Park

The landscape in Connemara, in the west of County Galway, has an almost mythical beauty. Between the Twelve Bens and the Maumturk Mountain ranges peat bogs stretch out, framed on three sides by a delicately indented coastline with myriads of little islands. in 1980, a strip of land measuring around 20 square kilometres / nearly eight square miles on the northwestern slopes of the Twelve Bens was declared a National Park, with the aim of preserving this landscape of heathland and bogs, typical of western Ireland, in its natural state. At 718 metres / 2,356 feet, Benbaun is the highest of these twelve peaks. The lower slopes were populated in the past, as witnessed by a number of decayed ruins. Connemara is considered a stronghold of the Irish (Gaelic) language: Irish-language radio and television stations transmit from here too.

## At a glance

**Location:** Connemara in the west of Ireland, in County Galway, north west of the Twelve Bens
**Area:** 20 km² / 7.7 mi²
**Foundation:** 1980
**www.connemaranationalpark.ie**

The national park owes its geological formation to the sediments from a warm primordial ocean. While heathlands were developing in the sparsely populated valleys, the Twelve Bens and the Maumturk Mountains remained almost bare.

The National Park was founded and opened to the public in 1980. A large portion of the area had previously been farmland belonging to the Benedictine Kylemore Abbey. The 445 metre / 1,460 feet-high Diamond Hill near Letterfrack affords the best view over Connemara.

# BALLYCROY
## National Park

The park occupies around 118 square kilometres / 46 square miles and accommodates the largest intact raised bog in Europe, the Owenduff Bog. Its significance as an ecological niche for numerous animals and plants is so great that the conservation and safeguarding of this unique bog land is considered of "international importance" according to the European Union. Hence this, the most recent national park in the country, was founded in 1998. Until that time, the area had been largely used for agricultural purposes as well as leisure activities such as hunting, fishing and mountain climbing. This had resulted in soil erosion and fish mortality. Apart from the bogs, other important habitats are conserved in the park, such as heathlands and fishing areas. Two of the largest rivers are the Owenduff and the Tarsaghaun River, both of which flow into the sea to the northwest of Ballycroy.

## At a glance

**Location:** County Mayo in the north west of Ireland
**Area:** 118 km² / 46 mi²
**Foundation:** 1998
**www.ballycroynationalpark.ie**

The National Park features vast wetlands scarps and river habitats.
The wetlands include the largest expanse of peat bog still preserved in Europe.

The Owenduff River is also an important conservation area because it is the only river in Western Europe that still supplies drainage to a relatively intact and extensive bog system. Many bird species have made their home around it (top: dunlins, dippers and redshanks). The golden plover also breed here; it appears in flocks as a winter guest (left).

# KILLARY HARBOUR AND
# MWEELREA MOUNTAINS

Killary Harbour is Ireland's only fjord. It stretches for about 16 kilometres / 10 miles from the mouth of the Erriff River near Leenane along the Atlantic on the west coast of Connemara. It was used by the British fleet as a naval base on a number of occasions because of its enormous depth. Most of the population of Killary Harbour live from salmon fishing. Rosroe Quay, near where the fjord opens into the sea, is a centre for salmon farming. At the youth hostel there, you will find a commemorative plaque to Ludwig Wittgenstein, who lived and worked in Rosroe Cottage in 1948. But it is not just anglers and fans of the philosopher who are attracted to Killary Harbour. Hikers, too, enjoy this deserted region, where the treeless mountain masses of the Mweelrea Mountains join up with the 814 metre / 2,670 feet main peak of the same name in the north.

## At a glance

**Location:** Killary Harbour is a fjord which ends in the north of Connemara and is connected to the Mweelrea Mountains
**Length:** 16 km / 10 mi
**Water depth:** 45 m / 148 ft
**Peak height:** 814 m / 2,670 ft

Rivers, streams, waterfalls and valley lakes surrounded by lofty mountaintops are what distinguish the fascinatingly diverse, largely uninhabited interior landscape near Killary Harbour. Doo Lough is a traditional trout fishing area.

# ACHILL ISLAND

At 140 square kilometres / 54 square miles, it is easily the largest island in Ireland and is connected to the mainland by a bridge. The inhabitants of Achill island spoke only in Gaelic until well into the 20th century and the old language is still maintained today in the eastern half of the island. In the 16th century, the pirate queen Grace O'Malley made use of the

remoteness of the island and set up a base in Kildavnet Tower on the east coast. Time and again, this inspiring landscape has also attracted artists. The Irish painter Paul Henry came for a short stay in 1910 - and remained for nine years.

## At a glance

**Location:** Achill, also called Acaill, an island in County Mayo, connected by the Michael Davitt Bridge to the mainland of the An Corrán peninsula
**Area:** 146 km² / 56 mi²
**Population:** 2,700 inhabitants
**www.visitachill.com**

# GLENVEAGH
## National Park

The territory of the national park, extending over the base of Mount Errigal, is primarily intended to be a home for endangered species, such as rare varieties of red deer and golden eagles. There are no trails across this lonely area. It was originally tilled by 244 tenants who were evicted in 1861 by John George Adair, the original owner - allegedly because of a plot but in fact it seems the tenants stood in his way, preventing him from realising his private plans. He had the magnificent Glenveagh Castle built on the site in the 1870s. After his death, his widow laid out gardens and brought in red deer. In the 20th century, Henry P. McIlhenny, an American of Irish origin, acquired the estate and extended the park. He left the property to the state and thus it was possible to open the park (1984) and the castle (1986) to the public.

## At a glance

**Location:** County Donegal
**Area:** 170 km² / 66 mi²
**Foundation:** 1984
**www.glenveaghnationalpark.ie**

In the centre of the National Park stretches Lough Veagh, which is around five kilometres / three miles long, on the shores of which John George Adair had Glenveagh Castle built as a neo-Gothic hunting lodge.

The National Park is an important nature reserve. A variety of vegetation zones, with plants such as the red foxglove (far left), are found in the sometimes densely wooded valleys with their lakes and peaks. A number of tours through the rough terrain of the park are offered.

# DONEGAL COAST

The name Donegal means "Fort of the Foreigners" and refers to the Vikings, who erected a fort in the bay. The biggest attraction of the small town is the ruins of Donegal Castle in its centre; this dates back to the 15th century. Only ruins remain, too, of Donegal Abbey, the former Franciscan monastery at the mouth of the Eske River. An obelisk at the Diamond, the triangular marketplace, commemorates the monks who wrote the historical work known as the "Annals of the Four Masters". Holidaymakers are particularly impressed by the west coast. At low tide, you can stroll across from Naran Strand on the promontory of Dawros Head to the north of Ardara to the tiny island of Inishkeel - there you will find the remains of an early Christian abbey. The coast now becomes more and more rugged, with innumerable offshore islands. It is certainly clear why the region north of Dungloe is called "The Rosses"; that is, the promontories. A ferry sails from Burtonport to the densely inhabited island of Aran.

**If you are making a tour around the northwest region of Donegal, it is worth making a detour to the beaches and harbour at Horn Head, with the broad view from its 180 metre / 590 feet-high cliffs.**

## At a glance

**Location:** County in the province of Ulster, near the tip of Donegal Bay
**Area:** 265 km² / 105 mi²
**www.donegaltown.ie**

### Fanad Peninsula

The narrow promontory of Horn Head juts out into the sea to the north of Glenveagh National Park and is bordered on the east by Sheephaven Bay. Seen from the distance, the cliffs have a distinctive blackish colouring due to their sparse vegetation. A hiking trail leads from the small town of Dunfanaghy through the bird sanctuary along the cliffs. On a clear day you can see Tory Island and the Rosquill peninsula from there. The Fanad peninsula lies to the west of Rosquill. The frigate "Saldana" was wrecked on Fanad's prominent crag in 1812. In 1814, as a result of this and at the request of Captain Hill of the Royal Navy in Derry, it was decided that a lighthouse would be built. It was lit in 1817. Since then, the lighthouse has been visible from afar and has become a world famous subject for postcards and calendars. It is possible to visit the upper platform for a fee. At 363 metres / 1,191 feet, Knockalla Mountain is the highest natural peak on Fanad. In 1607, the "Flight of the Earls" from the English colonialists took place from the village of Rathmullan, which is on Fanad. The peninsula was previously a salmon fishing centre, but the people there now live from tourists who appreciate that the fabulous Stocker Beach is one of Europe's most beautiful strands.

### Rosguill Peninsula

Rosguill peninsula is one of the four peninsulas which extend out into the Atlantic in the north of County Donegal. Unfortunately, it is often overlooked in favour of its larger sisters, Fanad and Inishowen, although Rosguill actually offers everything one might expect from the Emerald Isle. Coming from the south, one reaches Rosguill over a narrow headland where the village of Carrigart is to be found. The village is the access point for the Rosguill peninsula and the largest village in the Mevagh region, which includes Rosguill and the mainland to the south of it to the end of Mulroy Bay. The seaside village of Downings in on the peninsula itself. The Atlantic Drive starts here; this is a 12 kilometre / seven and a half mile-long ring road over which you can explore the Rosguill peninsula to the north as far as Melmore Head. The rugged coastal landscape of heather, grassland and rocks is watched over by Melmore Tower, an old outlook post on the knoll between Crocknasleigh and Melmore Head. The Atlantic Drive follows the cliffs, which drop steeply into the bay, providing a magnificent view of the Atlantic, the bay and Horn Head in the west.

### Inishowen Peninsula

The northernmost point of the peninsula is Malin Head. At Mamore Gap, the roads wind steeply up to a mountain pass at 240 metres / 788 feet, revealing a breathtaking panoramic view over the entire northern coast. The wild, rugged coastline around the northern tip is evidence of the vigour with which the Atlantic tides have shaped the land for eons. It marks the tip of the Inishowen peninsula, the largest peninsula in Ireland. This squeezes out into the sea between the inlets of Lough Swilly in the west and Lough Foyle in the east to the north of city of Derry. Its hilly interior with Slieve Snaght ("Snow Mountain"), rising to 600 metres / 1,968 feet, as its highest peak is practically unpopulated. Rows of fishing villages line the coast. A scenic route runs around the peninsula for around 160 kilometres / 100 miles. It begins in the east in Fahan and goes past a well preserved 17th century fortified tower in Buncrana northward - towards Carndonagh, where one of the oldest high crosses in Ireland was discovered. There is another cross on the peninsula at Culdaff.

# DONEGAL COAST

## Slieve League

The fascinating cliff landscape of Slieve League extends out over the Atlantic between Killybegs and Glencolumbkille. At exactly 601 metres / 1,972 feet, these cliffs are some of the highest in Europe. A narrow trail leads over the rugged crags, which basically necessitates good footgear and surefootedness. This "One man's path" begins at 300 metres / 984 feet at Bunglass Point, eight kilometres / five miles south of the village of Teelin. Right from the starting point, you have a view of the entire range of cliffs. The path leads further for a tour over the crest of the cliffs to Malin Beg, which takes about two hours. If that is too dangerous for you, you can go for the worm's eye view, which is still pretty impressive. Tourist boats start out from Killybegs, departing for the stretch of coastline below Slieve League.

**If you are lucky you may be able to observe seals diving if you explore the cliffs by boat (possible between April and October). It is important to look carefully since sea lions can dive as deep as 200 metres / 656 feet.**

They are truly steep and very high - the Slieve League cliffs tower exactly 601 metres / 1,972 feet above the blustering Atlantic Ocean. In the evening sun they are brilliantly lit in shades of orange or even fire-red.

# GIANT'S CAUSEWAY
## UNESCOWorld Heritage Site

The main attraction of the Causeway Coast is the Giant's Causeway, which can be reached from Bushmills by a heritage railway. The natural wonder is called the Giant's Causeway after one of the many legends which surround this location. The story tells of the Irish giant Finn, who, on being challenged by an opponent, built a causeway across the sea to Scotland, where there are similar basalt stones on the island of Staffa. Scientists have a more so-ber explanation for this natural wonder, which was declared a World Heritage Site by UNES-CO in 1986. According to them, it came about some 60 million years ago through processes of crystallisation as subterranean eruptions of lava streaming out into the sea slowly cooled. Around 40,000 of the basalt columns, stretch-ing up to six metres / 20 feet high remain, looming from the sea and forming a five kilo-metre / three mile-long projecting landmass.

## At a glance

**Location:** north coast of County Antrim, east of Bushmills, around 80 kilometres / 50 miles from Belfast
**Area:** 0.7 km² / 0.27 m²
**UNESCO-World Natural Heritage Site:** since 1986

The Giant's Causeway looks like a gigantic flight of stairs constructed by human hands. Among the predominantly hexagonal basalt columns, there are also stones with four, five and even eight sides.

John D Sutter is touring the island of Ireland in a clockwise direction for CNN. His description of the Giant's Causeway hints at the magical: "A golf-course green canyon wall slopes into a set of volcanic rock formations that are completely surreal: Near-perfect hexagonal tubes are stacked next to each other like puzzle pieces."

# ANTRIM COAST

To the east of the Causeway Coast is the north coast of County Antrim, from where you can see the Scottish peninsula of the Mull of Kintyre, only a few kilometres / miles away. The hook-shaped Rathlin Island, a rocky birds' paradise, lies just off its northernmost point, Fair Head, which is very popular with free climbers. Hikers especially appreciate this stretch of coast because of the often almost deserted Glens of Antrim: these nine valleys transect the high green plateau inland from the sea side, from Ballycastle in the north to Larne in the south. Each glen has its own individual character; the only thing they have in common is that they were formed by lava flow during the retreat of the glaciers. In spring, the flower-carpeted landscape is fed by numerous stream and waterfalls which gush from the crests of the hills into the valleys.

## At a glance

**Location:** historic region of County Antrim
**Length:** 50 km / 31 miles

# SHETLAND
## UNESCO Global Geopark

If you love the Scots, you absolutely must visit the Shetlands. The inhabitants here don't see themselves as Scottish and most certainly not as British. They are Shetlanders. Everything here is different. The climate: the winters are long but mild and the summers are short and cool. The light: in summer it never gets dark. The fauna: the famous ponies are here of course, but also whales and an endless number of seabirds. The language: if the Norwegian King Christian I had not given away the 100 or so islands (16 of which are inhabited) in 1469, they would still be part of Scandinavia. That history, however, still lingers. The old Nordic language can be heard everywhere - in practically every place name and in the regional dialect, spoken with that typically Scandinavia lilt. The section of cliffs through an extinct volcano near Eshaness, within the Geopark, is particularly worthy of mention.

## At a glance

**Location:** covers the entire Shetland archipelago off the north coast of the Scottish mainland
**Foundation:** 2000
**Designation as UNESCO Global Geopark:** 2015
**www.shetlandamenity.org**

# SHETLAND
## UNESCO Global Geopark

A trip along the Antrim Coast Road is only surpassed by a hike through the Glens of Antrim. White Park Bay is a swimming paradise, the unusual rock formation offshore are like natural stone bridges.

Little more than 22 centimetres / eight inches long, the sanderling is a wading bird of the sandpiper family. They appear on Rathlin Island in winter in particular, sometimes in large flocks.

If it's palm-lined, white-sand beaches you're after, the Shetlands are not for you. They are primarily rugged. But in turn you get an amazing cultural mix and peace. If you are the kind of person who would enjoy sharing all this with millions of seabirds, you're in the right place.

The cliffs are host to multitudes of nesting seabirds including fulmars, gulls, cormorants and puffins. Most of these migrate further in autumn; after that only gannets are to be seen on the craggy shores among the crustaceans. These are, by the way, a traditional Scottish dish. The sea is clean here; lobsters and shell fish are of very high quality.

# SHETLAND
## UNESCO Global Geopark

### Fair Isle

Fair Isle is remote from the rest of the Shetland Islands. Since 1954, it has belonged to the National Trust of Scotland, a private foundation, whose purpose is to preserve and maintain both the cultural heritage and the natural monuments. The tiny island is just three kilometres / one and a half miles wide by five kilometres / three miles long and it features bog landscape in the north and cliffs of up to 200 metres / 656 feet high on the west coast. There are around 70 people living here, most of whom grow their own vegetables. Aside from that, they have sheep; lots of sheep. And this is good, because Fair Isle is still most famous for its sweaters and their very distinctive patterns. These products are an important source of income for the islanders, alongside fishing. Nowadays, they even sell books on Fair-Isle knitting.

Locals like to refer to the rutted crags of Noss island with their small caves as "skyscrapers" because of the birds which live there in their thousands, such as puffins (top right) and northern gannets (bottom right).

## Noss

No people live on the isle of Noss, which occupies an area of around three square kilometres / just over one square mile off the south coast on Mainland. But umpteen thousand seabirds make their home in and on the cliffs. Common guillemots are the largest group. Gannets and the pretty puffins with their bright orange-coloured beaks are also to be seen in large numbers. A dinghy travels over regularly from the neighbouring island of Bressay. A tour around Noss takes four hours, during which you can see the highest point, the Noup at 181 metres / 594 feet. Depending on the time of year, you may also have to defend yourself from aggressive gulls who are protecting their brood. In early summer cotton grass dots the bog with white spots; heathers and different varieties of clover and orchid form carpets of pink and yellow flowers.

# SHETLAND
## UNESCO Global Geopark

This bird haven has only around 1,000 inhabitants. Seals, dolphins, porpoises and otters live in the surrounding waters. Thousands of northern gannets reside on a cliff in the Herma Ness bird sanctuary.

## Unst: Hermaness Nature Reserve

About one degree latitude further north than the Orkneys lie the Shetlands, with Unst at the northernmost tip. The island is full of varied landscapes with cliffs, sheltered coves and sandy beaches, heather hillocks and grey rocky wastes. The Hermaness Nature Reserve hosts hundreds of thousands of seabirds, including puffins, red-throated divers and great skuas -

the second-largest colony of this rare species of skua in the world lives on these cliffs. Botanists also often come here on tours of discovery; the isle is home to around 400 different plants. Other highlights are the 16th century Muness Castle and the old Boat Haven, with its traditional fishing boats and an exhibit on the subject of seafaring - if you are lucky, you may meet an old fisherman acting as museum attendant and will have the chance to listen to his old "seaman's yarns".

Every year 16,000 pairs of gannets and more than 50,000 puffins come to Hermaness to nest on the rocky vaults which tower up out of the sea.

# ORKNEY ISLANDS

Of the 70 Orkney Islands, situated off the north coast of Scotland, 18 are inhabited. Despite the fact that they are situated so far north, the Gulf Stream creates an unusually mild climate which favours agriculture, fisheries and tourism equally. Mainland, Hoy and South Ronaldsay are among the larger islands of the archipelago, the undulating landscape of which was formed by the glaciers of the last Ice Age. The island of Mainland, with its pre-historic finds, including Maeshowe, a stone Age tomb, is remarkable. Among the inscriptions there are three carvings created by Vikings showing a walrus, the head of a dog with its tongue sticking out and the so-called Maeshowe dragon, a sophisticated representation of a dragon with a sword in its back. This Maeshowe dragon is today one of the best-selling motifs used in the island's prospering jewellery industry.

## At a glance

**Location:** north of Caithness, within sight of the northern Scottish coastline, separated from it by the Pentland Firth
**Area:** 990 km² / 382 mi²
**www.visitorkney.com**

Otters (large picture) are picky animals, which means that wherever they live the natural ecology is intact – ideal conditions then, for other rare animals such as short-eared owls, Eurasian curlews and ravens (pictured left from top).

The cliffs and shallows off Marwick Head on the Orkney island of Mainland are treacherous. The ship MS Hampshire fell victim to them in 1916 and sank there. Among the passengers was Lord Herbert Kitchener, then Minister of War; a memorial was erected in his memory.

# ST KILDA
## UNESCO World Heritage Site

Of volcanic origin, the archipelago was spared from glaciation during the last Ice Age and hence retained its distinctive landscape. The archipelago "at the end of the world" includes Dùn, Soay, Boreray and the island of Hirta, whose inhabitant were evacuated in 1930. The islands have been uninhabited since then and nature has been left to its own devices. Dramatically precipitous cliffs provide nesting sites for rare bird species such as puffins. Despite their harsh climatic conditions, these islands were inhabited as far back as 2,000 years ago. The most remarkable structures are the cleits - a total of 1,430 have been found. These are small, stone-walled structures topped off with a large, grass-covered stone roof. They were mainly used for storing eggs, feathers and turf. In the modern era, people lived mostly on the main island of Hirta in natural stone cottages.

## At a glance

**Location:** the seven islands are around 64 kilometres / 40 miles west-northwest of North Uist in the North Atlantic
**Area:** 8.5 km² / 3.3 mi²
**UNESCO World Natural and Cultural Heritage Site:** since 1986

St Kilda is a haven for birds such as the delicately marked puffin and the gannet. The typical rock formations in the middle of the roaring Atlantic are known as "Stacks" (bottom).

There is space here for enormous gannet populations, and the seven islands of St Kilda form one of the world's most important breeding grounds for puffins.

# ISLE OF SKYE

The largest island of the inner Hebrides has become more popular than ever now that there is a bridge linking Skye directly to the Scottish mainland from the village of Lochalsh. At almost 1,735 square kilometres / 670 square miles, it is twice the size of the Baltic Sea island of Rügen; Skye features outstanding opportunities for hiking on its southern side. There are close to 10,000 people here, and they earn their living mainly from tourism. The island was given the name Sküyo ("Cloud Island") by the Vikings. In the Gaelic language it is known as Eilean Sgiathanach, the "winged isle", because of its irregularly indented coastline, or, depending on the weather, Eilean a Cheo, "Cloud Island". Nearly 60% of the inhabitants still speak this language; there is even a centre for Gaelic courses. In 1746, at the Royal Hotel in Portree, Bonnie Prince Charlie said farewell to Flora McDonald, who is still seen as a heroine today.

Skye is an enchanting landscape of endless moorlands, weirdly-shaped peaks and a spectacularly ragged coastline. The island is divided into five peninsulas: Sleat, Minginish, Duirinish, Waternish and Trotternish.

## At a glance

**Location:** directly off the west coast of the Scottish mainland in the Atlantic
**Area:** 1,735 km² / 670 mi²
**www.skyelive.co.uk**

Originally there were two breeds of Highland Cattle; the black and somewhat smaller Kyloe which lived on the islands in northwestern Scotland and the redder-coloured and somewhat larger breed from the remote highlands. The two types were bred together to produce one variety and acquired the red-brown colour which predominates today.

Dawn sheds a pink glow over the rocky
mountain landscape of Cuillin Hills on Skye.
The highest elevation is the 992 metre / 3,255
feet-high Sgurr Alasdair in the Black Cuillins.

# INVERPOLLY
## Nature Reserve

If the rising sun is not hidden behind clouds it paints an enchanting play of colour on the crags. Red deer can often be observed; they are less shy here because of the undisturbed nature of this sanctuary (right).

Secluded islands and rugged rocks form this somewhat remotely located mountain region of Inverpolly, about 30 kilometres / 19 miles north of Ullapool. The region was declared a nature reserve in the 1960s and is absolutely worth making a detour to see. Because if you have a soft spot for the north, you will love the Inverpolly Reserve in Scotland. Exciting paths wander through the different landscapes consisting of mountain, bog, woodland and lakes; for example the one point six kilometre / one mile-long nature trail which starts right by the Visitor Centre. Badgers, deer, otters and more than 100 varieties of bird live in this nature reserve. The alpine flora of this beautiful region is also especially biodiverse. Locals offer boat excursions and will tell you about the multifaceted landscape. Stac Pollaidh (590 metres / 1,936 feet) provides a good overview, hikers can reach its summit quite quickly from the car park at Loch Lurgainn. Geologists are most drawn to Knockan Cliff because the sequence of rock strata is reversed there due to tectonic movements.

## At a glance

**Location:** 30 km / 19 mi north of Ullapool, for many years the area was declared a National Nature Reserve but this designation has been limited to Knockan Crag since 2004.

# AN TEALLACH MOUNTAINS

Ten peaks stand in a semi-circle near the west coast of the Northwest Highlands, the highest of them break the 1,000 metre / 3,280 feet barrier. Rock climbers classify the An Teallach Mountains as one of the most challenging climbs in the British Isles. They can of course be mastered, but you need not only to be in excellent condition but also to have extensive experience and be surefooted enough to scale up the sharp sandstone ridge and trek around it. Good equipment is, naturally, a requirement on this jagged, treacherous ridge. All the more so in winter when snow conceals hollows or stumbling blocks, or during thaws when the moorland in the forests, from whence many people start their hike, is slippery and you sink deep with every step. An easier alternative leads just to the two Munros.

## At a glance

**Location:** in Western Ros in the Highland Council Area, in the northern part of the Fisherfield Forest
**Altitude:** 1,062 m / 3,484 ft

Quite a few Scottish mountain trekkers will tell you that the An-Teallach traverse is the most beautiful but also the most difficult mountain hike in the country–with a fabulous view over rugged, deeply carved valleys.

The An Teallach Mountain range initially climbs gently from the Fisherfield Forest moorland. Its pitfalls only become apparent in the vertiginous heights, especially in winter (left).

# NORTHWEST HIGHLANDS
## UNESCO Global Geopark

## At a glance

The North West Highlands Geopark is at the extreme north of the Scottish Highlands. Beginning with the Summer Isles in Wester Ross, near the busy ferry and fishing village of Ullapool which is one of the entrances into the park, the area covers over 2,000 square kilometres / 772 square miles of mountain, peatlands, beach, woodland and coast over West Sutherland and further to the north coast. The eastern border of the Geopark extends over the village of Durness and Loch Eriboll, and follows the Moine Thrust Zone, an internationally significant geological structure which helped 19th century geologists to discover how the great mountain ranges of the world were formed. This complex geology created breathtaking landscapes in which every type of rock generates its own unique and striking habitat.

**Location:** from the Summer Isles in Wester Ross via West Sutherland to the north coast
**Area:** 2,000 km² / 772 mi²
**Designation as UNESCO Global Geopark:** 2015
**www.nwhgeopark.com**

An excursion to Glen Torridon is like a journey back into Scotland's prehistory. The Torridon Hills are composed of a variety of sandstone. They are some of the oldest rocks and sit atop even older rocks, Lewisian gneiss.

Scotland's geology is enthralling and began 650 million years ago. The remains of the oldest known rocks in the world - Lewisian gneiss, named after the place they were found - can still be found today along the coast.

# WESTER ROSS
## UNESCOBiosphere Reserve

Formerly known as Beinn Eighe, Wester Ross Biosphere Reserve is in northwestern Scotland. It presents a range of habitats which are predominantly influenced by highland and oceanic factors. Most of Wester Ross is covered in open heathland areas, bare rock and wet grassland with scattered moorland. The forest, which is below 300 metres / 984 feet near Loch Maree, the fourth largest freshwater lake in Scotland, and lies in a variety of isolated ravines, contains the best preserved western pines in Great Britain as well as birch, hollies, ivy, rowans and junipers. The vast rocky mass of the 981 metre / 3,219 feet-high Slioch towers over Loch Maree in the southeast. Loch Maree is considered one of Scotland's most beautiful lakes, although it is also said to have its own monster: Muc-Sheilch is allegedly related to Nessie.

Wester Ross is dominated by wildly jagged rocks, remote valleys and long, steep slopes. The region features fast flowing rivers which open into secluded bays.

Rocky landscapes alternate with lakes and rich green meadows, but even the purple heather copes with the acidic peat soil. In olden days the stems were used to make ropes or it was used as insulation between stone walls. These days it is used as a source of dye and even for beer making.

## At a glance

**Location:** in the northwest of Scotland
**Area:** 5,299 km² / 2,046 mi²
**Designation as UNESCO Biosphere Reserve:** 1976
**www.westerrossbiosphere.com**

# WESTER ROSS
## UNESCO Biosphere Reserve

### Beinn Eighe National Nature Reserve

With its collection of mountains, old pine forests, secretive crossbills and soaring golden eagles, it is no wonder that Beinn Eighe was Great Britain's first National Nature Reserve. It was founded in 1951 and extends from the lakeside to the mountain top over an area of 48 square kilometres / 19 square miles. The centrepiece is the Beinn-Eighe Ridge - a group of craggy summits, spurs and screes between Loch Maree and Glen Torridon. The lower slopes accommodate remains of the old Caledonian pine forests.

The entire massif is a popular destination for hikers and mountain climbers. The Nature Reserve has a Visitor Centre on the southern bank of Loch Maree, on the east side of the massif.

On hot days, lake lovers from the surrounding villages of Torridon, Coulags and Achnasheen cool off in Loch Coulin after a boat trip; in the background, the imposing Beinn Eighe (large picture).

Some woodlands which include specimens of Scots Pine that are up to 350 years old have been preserved in the Biosphere Reserve. The stem and twigs of this silver birch (top right) are covered in moss. They are habitats for a multitude of species; for example you can find the mountain hare, pine marten (bottom right) and the red deer.

# WESTER ROSS
## UNESCO Biosphere Reserve

In the Highlands between the Isle of Skye and Ullapool you feel like you are at the end of the world. These are certainly among the least developed areas in Scotland, and yet the landscape here is particularly appealing.

### Loch Torridon

Torridon is an area of outstanding natural beauty which extends around the lakes of Torridon and Shieldaig and into the heartlands of Kinlochewe. Its unique combination of rocks and water make it special. Fishing has a long tradition here. As early as 1786 the first business was founded with the Torridon Fishery Company, but today only a few ruins remain as witness to that, on the Aird Mhoir peninsula on the south bank between Torridon und Shieldaig. Today, Loch Torridon is the location of a number of salmon farms.

### Loch Maree

The fourth-largest freshwater lake in Scotland has the typical long elongated shape of an Ice Age lake. There are 25 smaller and five larger islands in the lake, which is 25 kilometres / 15.5 miles long and up to four kilometres / two and a half miles wide. All of them are densely wooded. One of them, Maree Island, was the hermitage of St Maol Rubha, who founded a monastery at Applecross in 672. The ruins of a chapel, a holy well and an abandoned graveyard can be found there. The well water is said to have healing properties. The 981 metre / 3,219 feet-high rocky mass, Slioch, towers over Loch Maree in the southeast.

### Slioch

The view of the jagged stronghold of Slioch over the waters of Loch Maree is one of those classic vistas that is shown on calendars. The 981 metre / 3,219 feet-high peak is composed of Torridonian sandstone on a base of gneiss and has steep crags on three sides. Viewed from nearby Slioch presents a relatively easy ascent, considering its impressive appearance. The mountain can be reached easily from Kinlochewe. After around five hours, you will have finally crested the peak and can reward yourself with the view over Loch Maree and the Fisherfield Wilderness.

During the Middle Ages, red deer were driven over mountains and forests. The association between deer and the trees led to the term "deer forest" which is still found in the Highlands these days.

# RANNOCH MOOR

The Scots are a strong, tough breed of people who fear nothing and never back down. But there is one landscape to which even they capitulate - a nature that is so wild and indomitable that it cannot be subdued by man and cannot be cultivated under anyone's plough. And that's Rannoch Moor, one of the last untouched landscapes in Scotland, 130 square kilometres / 50 square miles of marshland in the Highlands, full of rivers, tarns, lakes and peat, and as black as night. 1,000 metre / 3,281 feet-high mountains surround this moor. The place has an eerie beauty; it seems to be stripped of all zest for life. "A wearier looking desert a man never saw", wrote Scottish writer Robert Louis Stevenson, author of "Treasure Island" in the late 19th century after a trip to Rannoch Moor.

## At a glance

**Location:** in the Highland, Perth and Kinross council areas and to a small extent in northern Argyll and Bute
**Area:** 130 km² / 50 mi²

The landscape at Loch na Stainge is characterised by warm autumn colours. Looking out from Rannoch Moor, your gaze can wander over the broad landscape, bordered on the horizon by the Black Mount range.

Lochan na h-Achlaise (far left), at nearly 300 metres / 984 feet above sea level, is one of the many lakes in Rannoch Moor. The moor can also be seen from the road: the A82 winds along the western edge until it drops in height shortly before Loch Tulla and merges into the landscape.

# GLEN COE

A pyramid as perfect as a pharaoh's tomb: the Buachaille Etive Mòr (1,022 metres / 3,353 feet high, all pictures) sits enthroned like a rocky lord over the valley of Glen Coe.

When the mist which is typical for this landscape rises and transforms the valley of Glen Coe (the village here is called Glencoe) into a mystical landscape, then one's thoughts may wander back in time to the infamous massacre of Glencoe in which dozens of men, women and children were murdered one winter night in 1692. Nowadays the valley is peaceful and very popular with hikers, who discover here a fabulous mountain landscape with rugged, snow-covered slopes, valleys eroded by glaciers, waterfalls, lakes, moors and tundra-like vegetation south of Ben Nevis, at 1,344 metres / 4,409 feet the highest mountain in the British Isles. Nevertheless, despite this natural idyll, one should never underestimate the rapid and unexpected weather changes which are typical of Scotland.

**The valley of Glen Coe has a wildly romantic beauty and is equally popular with lovers of winter sports, hiking and mountain climbing. The 2012 James Bond film "Skyfall" is one of a number to feature scenes shot here.**

## At a glance

**Location:** in the Highland council area, the starting point for visits is often nearby Fort William
**Length:** 16 km / 10 mi

# BEN NEVIS

At 1,345 metres / 4,411 feet, Ben Nevis is undisputedly the highest point in the United Kingdom. It consists of igneous rock that is around 400 million years old, dating from the Devonian period. Every year, it exerts an almost magnetic attraction, drawing around 100,000 hobby mountain climbers into the western Highlands. There are several ascent routes. They pass by sheep, a waterfall and a mountain lake. No matter which trail you chose, either a short, steep one with climbing passages or a long, moderate one, you will see the remains of an old meteorological station when you reach the summit. With luck, you will be able to savour the marvellous panoramic view. Unfortunately, fog often prevails over Scotland's highest point. It is not for nothing that Ben Nevis is also called "the mountain with its head in the clouds". It is better to leave it alone in winter and in summer to be prepared for all kinds of capricious weather.

The pride of the Scots, visible from a wide area, Ben Nevis, also known simply as "The Ben" is not only the highest mountain in their country, it is also the highest peak in United Kingdom.

Depending on the side from which one views the mountain it can be reminiscent of a camel's back. It is just as unpredictable as that desert animal and can readily throw off an incautious hiker.

## At a glance

**Location:** in the Scottish Highlands
**Altitude:** 1,345 m / 4,411 ft
www.ben-nevis.com

# CAIRNGORMS
## National Park

One minute the sun is beaming down and five minutes later it is pouring rain from heavy clouds. There is hardly a region in Europe where the weather changes so abruptly as in the Cairngorms. Maybe it is due to the mountains; five of the ten highest peaks in the British Isles are in this National Park. It is characterised by a subarctic climate; its Scot's pine forests and tundra-like environment provide a habitat for plovers and snow grouse as well as

for wildcats and pine martens. If you wish to explore nature, you need not dread long hikes through barren Scottish wildernesses - a cable car takes the visitor straight to the peak of Cairngorm. A glorious panoramic vista is revealed from there, over the precipitous mountaintops into which almost unspoiled valleys are sunk.

**With 49 "Munros" - the name for mountains in Scotland which are over 914 metres / 3,000 feet high - the "blue hills" (one translation of the Gaelic name Cairngorm) are truly spectacular (top).**

## At a glance

**Location:** in the central Highlands
**Area:** 3,800 km² / 1,467 mi²
**Foundation:** 2003
**www.visitcairngorms.com**

Diverse fauna: capercaillie (large picture), osprey, spotted woodpecker, squirrels and even reindeer (picture bar left) are just as at home here as cuckoos, brown owls, mountain hares and ptarmigan (picture bar right).

# LOCH TAY & TAY FOREST PARK

The little islands on Loch Tay are very striking. During the Ice Age, they were retreats for early settlers who sought refuge there from enemies. They constructed round houses on timber piles, known as crannogs.

The forests around the 23 kilometre / 14 mile-long lake are famous. Its waters reflect the trees, some hundreds of years old, and the barren peaks of the mountains. Before exploring the Nature Park around Loch Tay, the waters themselves deserve some attention. More specifically, the Isle of the Holy Women, the island where a convent of nuns once existed. This is no longer standing but one can visit the burial site of the wife of King Alexander I (1078-1124). And then off into the woods, which offer many vistas. The diversity of trees is impressive, as is their height. Red squirrels frolic in their branches, and if you hike through the woodlands at daybreak or dusk, you may be lucky enough to encounter a capercaillie or a fox.

## At a glance

**Location:** in the Scottish Highlands
**Area of Loch Tay:** 26 km² / 10 mi²
**Area of Tay Forest Park:** approx. 194 km² / 75 mi²
**www.visitscotland.com**

In some places the River Lyon snakes its way peacefully through floodplains and meadows, past towering spurs of the Grampian Mountains, some with weirdly-shaped crags.

# GLEN LYON

For some reason Glen Lyon tends to be somewhat overlooked, despite that fact that, at nearly 50 kilometres / 31 miles, it is Scotland's longest valley. It is not overrun by tourists streaming through here, and hardly any of the travel guides give it more than a few lines. This is a pity since this region, almost exactly in the heart of Scotland, is both diverse and attractive. On the one hand there are always weathered monuments, cosy teashops and even Roman bridges waiting to be discovered. On the other, some of the most famous Munros encircle the valley, those peaks which every Scottish Mountain climber is expected to scale. Not to mention the idyllic lakes, Loch Lyon and Loch an Daimh, embedded in the hilly landscape. They interrupt the furious upper courses of the river whose source is in the crags of Glen Lyon. Not far from there is Fortingall, a picture-perfect village.

## At a glance

**Location:** in the Scottish Highlands
**Length:** approx. 50 km / 31 mi
**www.visitscotland.com**

# ST ABBS AND EYEMOUTH
## Marine Reserve

The interplay between warm water and the cooler inflow from the Arctic creates a unique underwater environment. Certain types of coral require just this combination and so can be found here.

The waters on the coast of Berwickshire off the fishing village of St Abbs are regulated by the tides (the rhythm of the rising and falling sea). Hence it is home to an astoundingly large number of species. The St Abbs and Eyemouth Voluntary Marine Reserve was founded in 1984 to preserve this and to manage the difficult balancing act between the fishing industry and leisure activities in and on the water on the one hand and marine preservation on the other. It covers an area of over 10 square kilometres / four square miles. One of Europe's largest breeding grounds for seabirds such as kittiwakes and fulmars is found on the cliffs here. Starfish and lobster are among the creatures living underwater. They can be observed if you dive through the caves and rock tunnels. The kelp forests here are also fascinating for divers. This brown algae grows vertically up to eight metres / 26 feet high here.

Grey seals (large picture), starfish, lobster, Ballan wrasses and brittle stars (picture bar, from top) can also be encountered within the reserve.

## At a glance

**Location:** St. Abbs and Eyemouth Voluntary Marine Reserve, in the Scottish Borders Council Area
**Area:** 10 km² / 4 mi²
**Foundation:** 1984
**www.marine-reserve.co.uk**

# LOCH LOMOND & THE TROSSACHS
## National Park

In 2002, a national park occupying an area of nearly 1,900 square kilometres / 734 square miles at the point where the Lowlands merge into the Highlands was opened by Princess Anne. Its name indicates what it includes; that is, Loch Lomond, famous for its wooded shoreline areas and its islands and the hills of the Trossachs with their ancient woodlands. The forest area is in the eastern part of the park. The are numerous small lakes there too,

as well as mountains. But the highest elevation, the 1,174 metre / 3,852 feet-high Ben More, is in the north. It can be found in the park's third region, in Breadalbane. The fourth region is Argyll Forest Park. Leaving the Lowlands in the direction of the Highlands you will pass Loch Lomond. A rather heavily frequented road passes along its western shore. Hikers prefer the eastern shore, which provides more unspoilt nature and peace.

## At a glance

**Location:** geographically divided into four regions: Loch Lomond, the Trossachs, Breadalbane and Argyll Forest
**Area:** 1,900 km² / 734 mi²
**Foundation:** 2002
**www.lochlomond-trossachs.org**

The dense primordial woods and the many small lakes are referred to as the Trossachs. Loch Lomond is the largest lake in Great Britain. Who knows, you might even run into the Loch Lomond Monster here!

Rob Roy (Robert Roy MacGregor) is the hero of the Trossachs. The cattle dealer is also popularly known as the "Robin Hood of Scotland". His grave and an information centre focusing on his life can be found in the National Park.

# LOCH LOMOND & THE TROSSACHS
## National Park

### Falls of Dochart

Near the Killin bridge you can hear the sound of roaring and thundering. The Dochart waterfalls hurtle over rocky ground here - at least they do sometimes. At these times it is easy to appreciate how the first bridge, constructed in 1760, was torn down by floods. At other times the waters here can be astonishingly quiet and restrained as they thread through the rocks. This is what makes the rapids so attractive - they are never the same. After you have looked your fill on this wonder, you should turn around and cast your eyes downstream. There you will discover the island of Inchbuie, the ancient burial ground of the MacNab clan. The clan once held sway over nearby Killin, now famous for textiles.

### Ben A'an

Ben A'an is without doubt one of the most popular hills in the Trossachs. This is firstly due to its location close to Loch Lomond, and secondly due to the perfect hiking opportunities it offers. There are some passages with steep gradients but most of the paths are easy to walk. The open woods provide shade and an incomparable scent. You may cross a small mountain stream, and then stumble upon a great place to stop and rest. The last part has some rocky stretches. If you linger to the west of Loch Lomond, you can see the mountains in the distance.

### Loch Lomond

This, the largest lake in Great Britain, has even inspired a love song, which is often sung at the end of a convivial evening. Absolute peace can be found in the many tiny islands on Loch Lomond. Almost all of them are privately owned, but most are open for day trippers. The island of Inchconnach is especially popular. It has a population of wallabies which are a great attraction. These relatives of kangaroos were introduced in the 1940s by Fiona Bryde Colquhoun, later known as Lady Arran. Loch Lomond is one of the few places in the world outside Australia where these cute animals live in the wild.

Green, moss-covered crags, the roar of rushing water and just every now and then a beam of sunlight - it all adds up to an enchanting fairytale view. You might almost expect to meet an elf in this mystically atmospheric place.

### Loch Doine

The waters of Loch Doine flow through the Lairig before they drain into Loch Voil near Balvag. The village of Balquhidder lies to the north of Loch Voil. The old church has an irresistible attraction for visitors because of the grave of Rob Roy, the folk hero made famous by Sir Walter Scott. Even though it really attracts many people, both the church and also the entire region remain nonetheless pleasantly tranquil. Otters, martens and deer are at home all around the area of the Strathyre Forest, while squirrels scramble nimbly through the trees where buzzards, owls and eagles perch.

### Loch Voil

Loch Voil is a narrow lake, about five kilometres / three miles long. It is separated from Loch Doine by the Larig river and at its northern end drains into the Balvag near Balquhidder. The lake can be reached by a single-track road which leads from Balquhidder to Inverlochlarig. In Balquhidder, at the eastern end of Loch Voil, you can visit the grave of Scotland's Robin Hood, Rob Roy. A lookout point above the church, called the McLaren Stone, offers a panoramic view over Balquhidder Glen and along the full length of Loch Voil.

### Finnich Glen

With its moss-overgrown rock walls, quietly murmuring waters and its matchless air with the scent of pure nature, the steep gorge of Finnich Glen is bewitching. Slippery stone steps lead downwards, ferns sway in the breeze and gnarled old tree trunks invite you to take a rest. There are some steep passages which are slippery due to the constant moisture - these can only be tackled with a tensioned rope. No surprise, then, that not everyone is reminded of elves - the round platform-like rock in the middle of the gorge is known as the "Devil's Pulpit".

# GALLOWAY AND SOUTHERN AYRSHIRE
## UNESCO Biosphere Reserve

The natural area formed by the Galloway and Southern Ayrshire Reserve extends over 5,268 square kilometres / 2,034 square miles. It is based on the Galloway Hills, a water catchment area from which rivers running from the Highlands to the coast originate. This biosphere is characterised by the strong cultural and local identity of the area and a common thread of water connecting the natural environment, landscape and everyone living and working in the many small towns including Castle Douglas; Wigtown, Girvan, Maybole, Sanquhar, Cumnock or Dalmellington. The village of Glenlair is the home of James Clerk Maxwell (1831 - 1879), who discovered fundamental forces of natures through his theories on electromagnetism and light. Although heaths and patterned moorlands are actually rather unusual for the Highland location they are a valuable habitat for birds of prey, including golden eagles.

When the bluebells are in bloom, you know that spring has arrived on the island. There is a regular hype over these blue, bell-shaped flowers every year. The fact that their season only lasts for a few weeks gives them a special appeal.

## At a glance

**Location:** Highland massif in Merrick
**Area:** 5,268 km² / 2,024 mi²
**Foundation:** 1976 (as the Cairnsmore of Fleet and the Silver Flowe-Merrik Kells)
**Designation as UNESCO Biosphere Reserve:** 2012
**www.gsabiosphere.org.uk**

The biosphere is a valuable habitat for, among others, merlin, daylight hunting owls, sparrowhawks, spotted woodpecker and cuckoos (small pictures clockwise from top left). The deer in particular attract attention in autumn (left). Their roaring in the rutting season is unmistakeable.

# GALLOWAY
## Forest Reserve

The Nature Reserve - with its captivating, seemingly endless expanse - was founded in 1947. Some of the highest peaks in Scotland are situated within its 777 square kilometre / 300 square mile area which combines delightful valleys, picturesque lakes and mystical forests to produce a natural paradise. There are hardly any brightly lit buildings or other strong sources of light. This has made the Galloway Forest Park one of the three European National Parks with "Dark Sky" status. That means that details in the night sky which are obscured in cities, such as the belt of the Milky Way, are visible to the naked eye. If you have binoculars at hand you should be able to make out the rings of Saturn. On an earth-bound level, the nature reserve provides wonderful opportunities for hiking or mountain biking. Iron Age roundhouses are also worth a visit.

## At a glance

**Location:** Galloway Forest Park, in the heart of Galloway in southern Scotland
**Area:** 777 km² / 300 mi²
**Foundation:** 1947
**www.gallowayforestpark.com**

The park offers a vast range of landscapes from the coastal region to the mountain peaks. In addition it is sparsely populated, thus it provides optimum conditions for the wildlife to develop.

The hiker certainly need patience and a bit of luck to make out foxes, and red and roe deer between the dreamy ancient heather-carpeted rocks. Or you could just visit the local red deer and wild goat enclosures.

# NORTHUMBERLAND
## National Park

Danger lurked north of Hadrian's Wall in the past; today it is a place for stressed people to find heavenly tranquility. Northumberland National Park, between the Wall and the Scottish Border, is one of the most secluded spots in England. Even the hikers, nature watchers and mountain bikers don't get in each other's way. Now and again, however, you do come across evidence of the many borderland battles which have been fought here. The centre of the park is at the Kielder reservoir. Large open-air art installations lie in wait along the 44 kilometre / 27 mile-long Lakeside Way for hikers to find and enjoy. There is also an observatory, because the national park is also popular with astronomers. Far away from towns and other sources of artificial light, the dark night sky here glimmers with thousands upon thousands of lights.

## At a glance

**Location:** on the Scottish border
**Area:** 1,030 km² / 398 mi²
**Foundation:** 1956
**www.northumberlandnationalpark.org.uk**

Northumberland National Park is the ideal destination for those who love to explore regions which are off the beaten track. From wild goats to red foxes, there is an immense variety of animal life here.

Flora and fauna in harmony: rosebay willow-herb and blooming heather (left) grow here along with bog asphodel and pirri pirri with their ball-shaped flowers (top).

# NORTH PENNINES
## UNESCO Global Geopark

In the northern foothills of the Pennines lies the third largest nature reserve in England - it was also the first Geopark in the country because of its abundance of fascinating exposed stone strata. Visitors include not just hikers, cyclists, anglers and bird watchers - all fans of the outdoors can find lots to do here. There are special deals for horse riders, rock climbers, kayakers, sailing enthusiasts, survival experts, spelunkers, geologists, biologists, stargazers and even skiers. Towering majestically above it all sit  Cross Fell, Great Dun Fell und Little Dun Fell, the highest peaks of the Pennines. Although none of them reaches 900 metres / 2,953 feet high, they are covered with alpine vegetation and rare plants, often enveloped in clouds or buffeted by strong local winds. But if you ascend them in clear weather you will be rewarded with a view across the Solway Firth and all the way into Scotland.

## At a glance

**Location:** extends over large parts of the counties of Durham, Northumberland and Cumbria in the North of England
**Foundation:** 2003
**Designation as UNESCO Global Geopark:** 2015
**www.northpennines.org.uk**

This special place captivates its visitors with its breathtaking landscape made up of pretty hayfields, torrential highland rivers, beautiful forests, welcoming villages and fascinating traces of its mining past.

An example of spring gentian, yellow flowering biting stonecrop, blue meadow cranesbill and poppies (small pictures clockwise from top left) growing on a stone wall close to the picturesque village of Blanchland.

# NORTH PENNINES
## UNESCO Global Geopark

### River Tees

The Tees is one of the most spectacular rivers in England. It rises at 750 metres / 2,460 feet above sea level on the eastern slope of Cross Fell in the North Pennines and it runs to a plateau where it has been dammed to form the Cow Green Reservoir. The reservoir's construction was highly controversial; however you will still come across a wide range of alpine habitats around the lake which cannot be found anywhere else in England. These include bogs and heathlands, low-growing juniper scrubland, limestone grassland, rough grazing and alpine meadows. Where the river emerges from the reservoir the water falls in a succession of rapids down a valley. High Force waterfall produces the largest volume of water of any in England; water is catapulted straight out from a wall then gushes down over the wider Low Force to a whitewater area, an inviting place for an action-packed kayak trip.

Due to the different rock stratification, the river Tees washed out the softer sandstone faster than the hard dolerite rock. This gave rise to an overhang, or sill, and the eventual evolution of a gorge that is currently around 700 metres / 2,300 feet long.

At High Force waterfall, the Tees drops vertically about 21 metres / 70 feet. If you take the woodland walk from the Bowles Visitor Centre you can hear it rumbling.

# ISLE OF MAN
## UNESCO Biosphere Reserve

This island covers an area of 572 square kilometres / 220 square miles and its inhabitants are proud of their glens and valleys. Dhoon Glen has a wild side as well as a charming one. Moss-covered crags around 140 metres / 460 feet high tower almost vertically above the entrance to the valley. Two waterfalls tumble from the precipitous walls; locals call the larger of these "Big Girl". Some say that you can hear the wailing of a girl who drowned here once. There are generally reputed to be many ghosts, trolls and fairies situated on the island. For instance, the black dog, Moddey Dhoo, which is supposed to walk abroad in the ruins of Peel Castle on the west coast. The highest elevation on the hilly island is the 621 metre / 2,037 feet-high Snaefell. Those who crest the summit will have seven kingdoms at their feet: Man, Ireland, Scotland, Wales and England as well as the heavens and Neptune's kingdom.

## At a glance

**Location:** an island in the Irish Sea between England and Ireland
**Area:** 572 km² / 220 mi²
**Designation as UNESCO Biosphere Reserve:** 2016

The Isle of Man has a rocky coastline featuring high cliffs that are particularly spectacular. The Langness peninsula, which protrudes some two kilometres / over a mile, at the southern end is one of these. The name Langness comes from the old Nordic and means "long promontory".

Sunset in the coastal village of Port Erin on the south of the Isle of Man (left) casts a romantic glow over wood anemones (top right), roses and purple coloured autumn anemones (bottom right). But the moss-covered crags also have their own very special, if somewhat rugged, charm.

# LAKE DISTRICT
## National Park

This stunning landscape of mountains and lakes became famous in the 18th and 19th centuries through the writings of the "Lake Poets", including William Wordsworth. The area, covering some 2,300 square kilometres / 888 square miles and usually simply referred to as "The Lakes", starts around 130 kilometres / 80 miles northwest of Manchester. Trough valleys were formed here as a result of several ice ages, especially the last, the Weichsel Ice Age, which ended about 15,000 years ago. They give the national park its name. The Cumbrian Mountains make up a large proportion of the landscape. In the upper regions there are many glacial cirques with tarns, and the lower regions are dominated by extensive upland moors blanketed with bracken and heather. This landscape has had an inspiring effect ever since the 18th century, when the artists of the Romantic period dedicated their paintings and writings to it.

## At a glance

**Location:** in the county of Cumbria in northwestern England, around 130 kilometres / 80 miles from Manchester
**Area:** 2,300 km² / 888 mi²
**Foundation:** 1951
**UNESCO World Heritage Site:** since 2017
**www.lakedistrict.gov.uk**

The old stone Ashness Bridge is located in a wildly romantic spot on the single-track road from Borrowdale road in the direction of Watendlath in England's Lake District (large picture).

Lake Buttermere, in the valley of the same name, is justly popular with visitors; after all you can do a circuit of the lake in about three hours and discover some picnic sites along the way. In addition to the hiking trails around the lakes, there are also tracks leading up to the summits of Haystacks and Red Pine.

# Wildlife in the Lake District

Within the hilly landscape of the Lake District, numerous fish-filled lakes such as Buttermere and Crummock Water alternate with woodlands with extensively cultivated pastures and fields. Aside from robins, elk and roe deer, the national park also contains animals which are otherwise rarely sighted in Great Britain, such as the red squirrel and the buzzard-sized red kite. In 2007 the unmistakeable goshawk was voted the most popular bird by the people of Wales. Less than one hundred years ago, only two breeding pairs were to be found in the whole country. Although the species has recovered well since then, and several hundred can be sighted in the skies above the Lake District, the red kite is still classed as endangered. The same is true of the schelly, a salmon-like fish with small black markings on its back and sides. Its population occupies an area smaller than 20 square kilometres / eight square miles. You could say that the Lake District is an angler's paradise, but that is only true to an extent since angling is strictly regulated. You have to put up with quite a number of restrictions since, apart from the schelly, there are a number of other rare varieties of fish in the lakes. The use of freshwater fish as bait is, for example, strictly forbidden in 14 lakes. The main reason for this is to prevent any foreign species entering the lakes

Red kite pairs are faithful for years even though they don't spend the winters together. They find each other again when they return to their breeding ground. They build their nests in trees as high as 20 metres / 66 feet.

so that the fragile wildlife is preserved. If, during a visit, you need to pass the time on a rainy day, the Lakeside Aquarium on the shores of Lake Windermere, which portrays the diverse animal world of the Lake District is worth a visit. The instructive guided tours which are included in the entry price are also to be recommended.

Kingfishers, robins and bullfinches with their black heads and flanks (picture bar from top), are just as at home in the Lake District as the brown feathered curlew (left).

# YORKSHIRE DALES
## National Park

If you are looking for solitude and a vast, almost limitless view, you will love the Yorkshire Dales. Broad pastures seamed with ancient dry-stone walls are characteristic of the austere hilly landscape permeated with individual river valleys (dales) in the Pennines. If you climb out of these, you will come to a rugged karstic moor and heath landscape from which, every now and then, a storm-swept tree or weirdly-shaped rock looms. Most of the area is un-der protection as a national park. It is seen at its best in autumn with a hike on one of the numerous long-distance or circuit tracks when the blooming heather covers the hills with a deep purple shade. Among the valleys, Wensleydale is especially popular. This is home to the castle of the same name, the ruin of Bolton Castle, and the television series "All Creatures Great and Small".

## At a glance

**Location:** in northern England, flanked by the M6 to the west
**Area:** 2,025 km² / 782 mi²
**Foundation:** 1954
**www.yorkshiredales.org.uk**

Simply stunning - sunrise over the natural limestone formation of Malham Cove near the village of Malham in the Yorkshire Dales National Park.

Wensleydale is one of the most famous dales in the park. The imposing three-stage waterfall, Aysgarth Falls (top right), is situated there. But the West Burton waterfall (below), about 14 kilometres / nine miles from the village of West Burton, and the lovely Scale Haw waterfall (bottom right) near the charming village in Wharfe Valley are also worth a trip.

# NORTH YORK MOORS
## National Park

In the west, the hills of the North York Moors descend steeply into the sea. If you follow the coastline on the Cleveland Way from Scarborough to Redcar, your effort will be constantly rewarded by spectacular panoramas. But there are also good hikes inland. More than 2,000 kilometres / 1,243 miles of signposted paths thread through the national park. It is a deserted area with broad moorland and heath landscapes which are frequently dissected by rug-

ged rock formations and terrain faults. Driving here can be very arduous; it is more comfortable to travel on the heritage train which operates regularly between Whitby and Pickering in the summer. For mountain bikers, there is the Moor to Sea Cycle Network which allows you to create your own tours along the coast and straight through the national park.

## At a glance

**Location:** plateau in North Yorkshire in the northeast of England, southeast of Middlesbrough, directly on the North Sea
**Area:** 1,436 km² / 555 mi²
**Foundation:** 1952
**www.northyorkmoors.org.uk**

With its 13 kilometre / eight mile-long chalk cliffs, Flamborough Head is one of the most spectacular areas in the English coast of Yorkshire between the bays of Filey and Bridlington on the North Sea.

Meadow pipit and grouse (picture bar from top) feel particularly at home by the May Beck River and elsewhere in the North York Moors National Park.

# NORTH YORK MOORS
## Nationalpark

To the west of York, between the Lake District and the North York Moors, is the hiking paradise that is the Yorkshire Dales.

# PEAK DISTRICT
## National Park

Surrounded by the industrial cities of Manchester, Sheffield and Stoke-on-Trent, the Peak District is England's oldest national park. But city-dwellers initially had to assert their right to roam in the country. Their illegal Mass Trespass in 1932 led to this private property, mostly belonging the Duke of Devonshire, being opened to the public. Hiking is still the most popular sport in the Peak District, but cyclists, riders, rock climbers and paragliders also have

their stomping grounds here. Whereas the north, around the 636 metre / 2,087 feet-high Kinder Scout, the "Dark Peak", is characterised by broad heathlands and upland moors, lonesome summits and spectacular rock formations, the "White Peak" in the south has a delightfully green hilly landscape with limestone plateaus, wooded valleys and pretty little villages.

## At a glance

**Location:** Dark Peak is part of the Greater Manchester and Yorkshire counties; the White Peak area belongs in Staffordshire, Derbyshire and Cheshire
**Area:** 1,404 km² / 542 mi²
**Foundation:** 1951
**www.peakdistrict.gov.uk**

Castleton is a village in Derbyshire. Because of its location at the end of the Hope Valley in the Peak District National Park it is surrounded on three sides by mountains. The ruins of Peveril Castle tower majestically over the village.

The lovely little waterfall with its cascading water in the Padley Gorge, hidden in the woods near Grindleford, is a surprise to stumble on (far left).

# SHERWOOD FOREST

Exactly when the story of Robin Hood was told for the first time is lost in the mists of time. But certainly by no later than the 15th century every child in England knew the story of the great outlaw who stole from the rich to give to the poor. He is said to have lived in Sherwood Forest - once a mighty forest with stately oak trees - and repeatedly played tricks on the Sheriff of Nottingham. If you come to Sherwood Forest today, you will search in vain for the dense primeval forest with ancient trees whose leaves must have seemed to veritably rustle with history. There is barely 30 square kilometres / 12 square miles remaining of the once so proud forest to explore. But you can still experience some genuine Robin Hood atmosphere by the most important and largest oak, known as the Major Oak.

**The Major Oak, which stands very close to the village of Edwinstowe, is between 800 and 1000 years old.**

## At a glance

**Location:** surrounds the village of Edwinstowe in Nottinghamshire
**Area:** 30 km$^2$ / 12 mi$^2$
**www.sherwoodforest.org.uk**

The term forest is misleading, since large parts of Charnwood Forest have been deforested. Bare hills alternate with open grassland, picturesque rock formations, small areas of water and lightly wooded areas whose floor is carpeted in bluebells every spring. It is this very diversity which give this area of roughly 25 square kilometres / 10 square miles its special charm and also its ecological value. In earlier centuries the most challenging fox hunts in England took place here around the village of Quorn. Today it is the footpaths and climbing opportunities which draw people. On your way, you may stumble upon old quarries where stone for whetstones and millstones was once extracted. Popular places with public access are Bardon Hill, Beacon Hill, Bradgate Park, Swithland Wood, the Outwoods and Stoneywell Cottage.

Ancient volcanic rocks shape the landscape of Charnwood Forest, an area in Leicester. This is also where the first fossil of a prehistoric fern, approximately 500 million years old, was discovered.

# CHARNWOOD FOREST

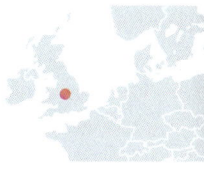

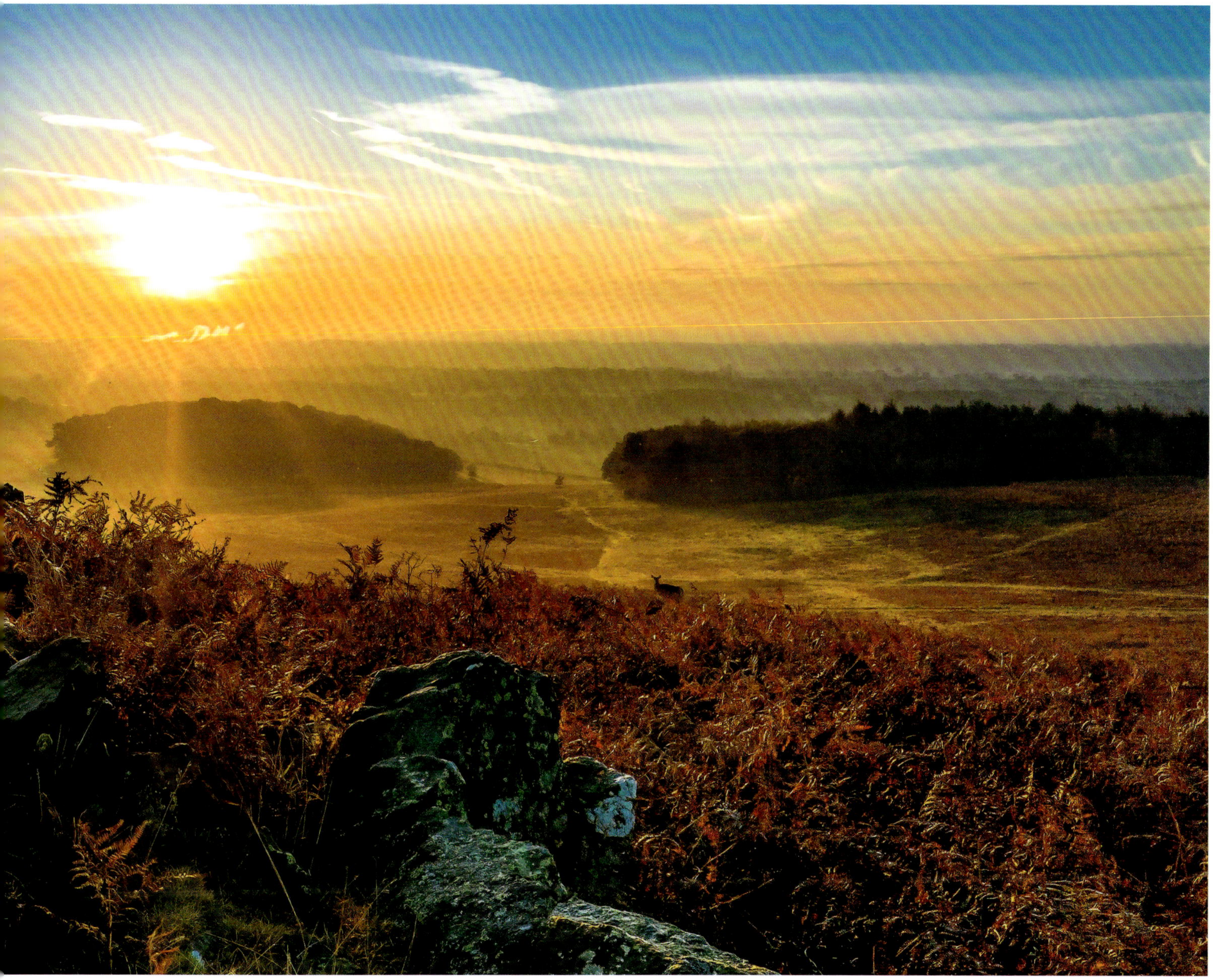

## At a glance

**Location:** upland tract in northwestern Leicestershire, bordered by Leicester, Loughborough and Coalville
**Area:** 25 km² / 10 mi²
**www.charnwood.gov.uk**

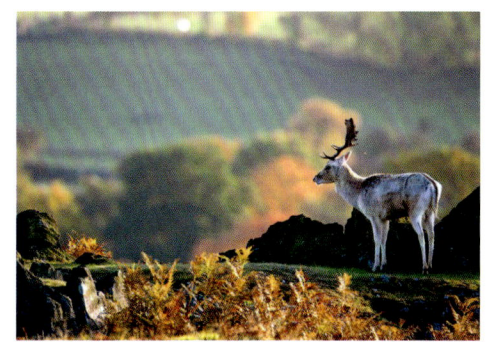

Viewed from the elevation in Bradgate Park, a part of Charnwood Forest, you can see all the way to Leicester if the sky is clear. Footpaths open up the landscape and lead to geologically important locations where numerous significant fossils have already been found. Fallow deer are among the fauna living in the nature reserve belonging to Charnwood (left).

# SHROPSHIRE HILLS

These hillocks in southwestern Shropshire are still considered peaceful and little explored. They differ drastically from the rest of the agricultural region. With Long Mynd and its narrow valleys, a long-extinct volcano raises its head not far from Bishop's Castle. The market town of Church Stretton with its mill valley (worth visiting) is in such a picturesque location, wedged between its hills, that it proudly bears the nickname "Little Switzerland". The rock formations known as the Stiperstones, which were created by weathering, run along an mountain ridge eight kilometres / five miles long and are also extremely distinctive. A lovely hiking path leads to the Devil's Chair and Shepherd's Rock at a height of 536 metres / 1,759 feet, where a magnificent view over the mythically beautiful hilly landscape is revealed.

## At a glance

**Location:** in the south of the English county of Shropshire, extending to the Welsh border
**Area:** 802 km² / 310 mi²
**www.shropshirehillsaonb.co.uk**

According to legend, the famous Stiperstones, an unusual rock formation in Shropshire, were made by the devil himself.

Green hills and sheep pastures as far as the eye can see. These are the hallmark of the Batch Valley in the Long Mynd heather and moor uplands near Church Stretton.

# NORFOLK COAST

The seemingly endlessly wide skies over Norfolk with their ever-changing moods offer peace and relaxation to stressed city dwellers. On beach walks you can experience the continual interplay of ebb and flood and, when exploring wetland areas, discover rare plants. When it comes to seabirds, there is hardly a place in England which has a greater diversity or offers better opportunities for observation. The continuous coastal hiking trail promises plenty of variety. You can tramp through the dunes at Holme-next-the-Sea, explore broad marshland to the east and revel in the view of the bluffs near Sheringham. It is all beautiful, precisely because the landscape doesn't push itself to the fore. The fresh, crisp wind is a significant factor and tempts you to fly a kite.

North Norfolk has an unparalleled coast with unspoiled, award-winning beaches, including Holkham near Hunstanton, Beach of the Year in 2018.

## At a glance

**Location:** the coastlines and farmland of the Wash in the west, to the sand dunes of Winterton in the east
**Area:** 450 km² / 174 mi²
**Foundation:** 1968
www.visitnorthnorfolk.com

North Norfolk is an area of outstanding natural beauty and is home to a large part of the Broads National Park, Great Britain's largest wetland with salt marshes. It makes North Norfolk a paradise for wildlife such as grey seals (left) and birds such as the snow bunting, knot and ruddy turnstone (picture bar from top).

# THE BROADS
## National Park

It is like another world - between Norwich and the coast, a landscape seamed with rivers, canals and small, shallow lakes which came about as a result of peat cutting in the Middle Ages. Numerous windmills attest to repeated efforts to drain the marshes. Nowadays, especially at weekends and in the summer holidays, the waters teem with thousands of sailing and motor boats and, increasingly, canoes. Hikes and cycle tours in the Broads are also full of charm. To conserve the unique nature of this water landscape with its rare plant species and many birds, the Norfolk and Suffolk Broads Act, giving the Broads equivalent legal status to the national parks in England and Wales, was enacted in 1988. The area was finally declared a national park in 2015.

## At a glance

**Location:** in the English county of Norfolk, about 13 kilometres / eight miles east of Norwich
**Area:** 160 km² / 62 mi²
**Foundation:** 2015
**www.visitthebroads.co.uk**

Kingfishers, bitterns and swans (small picture bar from left) live in the nature reserve. In summer, dragonflies dance above the orchid-filled meadows. And geese overwinter in the colder months - they can be observed in the Berney Marshes.

# SOUTH FORELAND AND HERITAGE COAST

White chalk cliffs and shingle beaches alternate on the coast of southeast England along the counties of Sussex and Kent and in between are famous seaside resorts such as Brighton and Eastbourne. The inland areas are charming, with hilly green scenery and delightful parklands. For those who love to wander in the footprints of history there are attractions such as the moated Leeds Castle, picturesque towns such Canterbury with its celebrated ca-

thedral and the cradle of Anglo-Saxon culture in Winchester. The South Foreland lighthouse in St Mary's Bay is Victorian, built in 1843, and was used by Marconi for the first radio ship-to-shore contact in 1899. At the foot of the lighthouse there are two lighthouse-keeper cottages in which whole families used to live. One of them is now a traditional tearoom.

## At a glance

**Location:** area in the southwest which extends from Dover half-way to Deal in Kent

The South Foreland lighthouse stands on the white cliffs of Dover on the western edge of St Mary's Bay. It was the first electrically operated lighthouse and also the scene of the first international radio signal transmission.

The spider orchid (left) is only found on the chalk cliffs of the south coast in Dorset. Its petals are yellow-green and arch inward towards the flower. The "head" of the spider has a pouch, the sides of which shine with nectar like spider eyes.

# BRIGHTON AND LEWES DOWNS
## UNESCO Biosphere Reserve

Founded in 2014, the Brighton and Lewes Downs biosphere reserve is in Sussex on the south coast of England near the city of Brighton and Hove. Forming a central unit of the hills of the South Downs National Park, it is on the Brighton chalk block that lies between the River Adur in the west and the River Ouse in the east. Extending over a number of kilometres / miles, the chalk downland makes up the principal terrestrial landscape. The coastline is dominated by impressive chalk cliffs and urbanised plains, running to the estuary of the River Adur at Shoreham-by-Sea. The reserve includes three distinct but interrelated habitats. Among others, it includes 20 different butterfly species. The wart-biter and adonis-blue butterfly are just as much at home here as the northern fulmar, hedgehog and yellowhammer.

## At a glance

**Location:** on the south coast of England, between the rivers Adur and Ouse
**Area:** 295.14 km² / 113.95 mi²
**Designation as UNESCO Biosphere Reserve:** 2014

Tranquility returns as soon as the sun sets in the area of the Brighton and Lewes Downs. The reserve welcomes around twelve million tourists every year, thanks to its scenic beauty and proximity to London.

In summer, while the bluebells are flowering in an oak wood near Brighton (far left), the venomous adder takes advantage of the warming sunrays to hatch its eggs. Unlike most other reptiles, which lay their eggs in the earth, the adder keeps its inside its body. The advantage of this is that it can creep around in search of the sun.

# SOUTH DOWNS
## National Park

White is a colour which nature reserves for special moments only - for the fleetingness of sea spray, the impermanence of snow or for salt, the elixir of life. For it to grant stone the colour of purity is an infrequent occurrence which makes the impression all the more overwhelming when nature for once demonstrates its generosity like this. She is her most benevolent at the chalk cliffs of southern England, the most spectacular part of which forms the South Downs in Sussex and Hampshire. In primeval times they rose out of a tropical sea and they are composed of millions of compacted skeletons of coral and crustaceans - their spotlessness gives the impression of a metaphor for eternity. Actually, though, their beauty is transitory. The stone is so soft that it cannot offer any resistance to wind and rain and is slowly sinking into the sea.

## At a glance

**Location:** in the counties of Hampshire, West Sussex and East Sussex in southern England
**Area:** 1,600 km² / 618 mi²
**Foundation:** 2011
**www.southdowns.gov.uk**

Eventually even the "Seven Sisters", the most distinctive formation in the South Downs between Eastbourne and Seaford, will also once more become water spirits because of the fragile nature of the limestone.

## Seven Sisters

These chalk cliff formations are situated between Eastbourne and Seaford in Sussex. The Seven Sisters are considered the most impressive cliffs in the South Downs coastal region. They form a spectacular cliff coastline which has been filmed, photographed and painted countless times. There are in fact now eight sisters, since a new cliff has been created by erosion. According to an exhibition at the National Trust Visitor Centre near Birling Gap, the name has existed since the 16th century. The eighth cliff was presumably formed more recently but the historical title has been retained. To the east of the last cliff is the village of Birling Gap, which is seriously threatened by erosion.

Describing the Seven Sisters, the British author Rudyard Kipling (1865 - 1936) wrote fondly of "our blunt, bow-headed, whale-backed downs".

## Beachy Head

The fascinating, scenic Seven Sisters Country Park, named after the seven bright white cliffs, starts just a little behind Eastbourne. A hike on the South Downs Way leads along the coast over the striking chalk cliff landscape. From Beachy Head, at 163 metres / 535 feet the highest chalk cliff in the United Kingdom, one has a breathtaking view over the English Channel and onto the famous Belle Tout Lighthouse, dating back over 115 years, in the sea. In 1999, because of advancing erosion, this was moved in one piece some way further inland to prevent it from falling into the sea. The postcard panorama of the Seven Sisters can however only be seen from the next cliff along, South Hill.

# NEW FOREST
## National Park

England clings to its traditions with an almost religious, single-minded earnestness. There are historical continuities here which would be unthinkable elsewhere. The New Forest in Hampshire, for example, is not a new forest but a very ancient one. William I of England, known as the Conqueror, had it declared a royal hunting ground as early as 1079. The inhabitants were driven out and strict laws put in place to protect the forest. In particular, venison from New Forest deer landed as a delicacy on the royal table and their antlers ended up in one or another of the monarch's castles. To this day the Crown still owns 90% of the New Forest, almost as if nothing has changed since the time of William the Conqueror. Only nature itself has changed; most of the trees have now given way to heathland.

## At a glance

**Location:** in Hampshire and a small part in Wiltshire in the south of England
**Area:** 571 km² / 220 mi²
**Foundation:** 2006
**www.newforestnpa.gov.uk**

Right in the centre of the densely populated southeast of England, idyllic grassland and peaceful heathlands can be found in the New Forest. Its 3,000 very special inhabitants, the New Forest ponies, are an indispensable, integral part of the national park.

The New Forest recreational area is barely a two hour train journey from London. The national park is one of the few areas in England where increasingly threatened landscape forms such as raised bogs and mires can still be found.

# CRANBORNE CHASE

The chalk plateau of Cranborne Chase and the West Wiltshire Downs extend across the south west of Wiltshire. Picturesque hiking and cycling routes invite you to explore the natural beauty of this diverse landscape. Right at the centre are the ruins of Wardour Castle, dating back to the 14th century, which was partly destroyed during the Civil War. As you explore the grottos and castle rooms, you may get the feeling you are in the Hollywood blockbuster Robin Hood (1991), because part of that film was shot here. The nearby nature reserve of Langford Lakes in the Wylye Valley between Salisbury and Warminster will also tempt you to linger, with its fascinating wildlife. Its four lakes offer vital habitation to 150 types of birds. Thus, in spring you can observe the great crested grebe as it shakes its head in its courtship dance.

## At a glance

**Location:** between the counties of Dorset, Hampshire and Wiltshire in the south of England
**Area:** 989 km² / 382 mi²
**Foundation:** 1975
**www.ccwwdaonb.org.uk**

The chalk plateau of Cranborne Chase straddles the counties of Dorset, Hampshire and Wiltshire. it borders on Salisbury Plain and the West Wiltshire Downs in the north and the Dorset Downs in the southwest.

The varied landscape of Cranborne Chase is situated near the border between Dorset and Wiltshire, where chalk escarpments rise steeply to the rounded crest of Breeze Hill.

# DORSET AND EAST DEVON COAST (JURASSIC COAST)
## UNESCO World Heritage Site

Sediments from the Triassic, Jurassic and Cretaceous periods present themselves like a cut-open sandwich on the Jurassic Coast, the spectacular coastal strip from Dorset to East Devon. The cliffs are petrified witnesses of the evolution, development and extinction of animal and plant species - not least the dinosaur. A type of dinosaur which only existed here was discovered in 2000. A chance find by a young girl at the beginning of the 19th century brought the area to the attention of geologists. She said that she had seen a dragon on the coast; in reality it was the first complete impression of an ichthyosaur. Even today one stumbles on traces of prehistory everywhere one walks. Erosion, especially after severe storms, is continually revealing new fossils.

## At a glance

**Location:** a section along the English Channel coast of southern England, from Orcombe Point in the county of Devon in the west to the Old Harry Rocks near Swanage in the Isle of Purbeck in the east
**Length:** 150 km / 96 mi
**UNESCO-World Natural Heritage Site:** since 2001

Unique jewels of geological history are buried here. The Jurassic Coast in the south of England was formed 185 million years ago and is one of the most significant fossil excavation sites in the world.

The coastline was not always the same as it is today. According to the theory propounded by some geoscientists, the impact of a large meteorite 65 million years ago created a massive tsunami and washed away terrestrial animals which one now finds as fossils.

The Jurassic Coast has been on the UNESCO World Heritage List since 2001. This natural stone arch on the coastal strip is named Durdle Door.

# DARTMOOR
## National Park

At 945 square kilometres / 365 square miles, Dartmoor National Park is an area of largely pristine woodland and moor on the southwest coast of England. The region lies almost 500 metres / 1,640 feet above sea level and is one of Europe's largest nature parks. Dartmoor is not a primeval landscape but has been cultivated for thousands of years. Numerous archaeological sites - the remains of Stone Age villages, stone rows and circles, monuments and burial tombs - attest to its settlement history. A hiking trail network around 800 kilometres / 500 miles long traverses the landscape; in some places the granite outcrops jut out from the landscape as rocky crests (known as Tors). Red-brown fern fronds, heathers, wind-swept bushes and shaggy Dartmoor ponies define the image of the national park, especially in the barren west.

## At a glance

**Location:** in the English county of Devon
**Area:** 945 km² / 365 mi²
**Foundation:** 1951
**www.dartmoor.gov.uk**

From rugged granite cliffs to deeply wooded river valleys, from heather-covered moors to sleepy villages - Dartmoor is a landscape of contrasts.

The 40 centimetre / 16 inch-high red grouse (far left) lives on heathland where cranberries and bilberries are found. Also diurnal and territorial is the common lizard (left), which likes to bask on the granite crags in the national park.

# CORNWALL COAST

The Bedruthan Steps cliff formation (top) received its name from the notion that the giant Bedruthan of English legend used to use these large stone as steps.

Rosamunde Pilcher, whose Cornwall-based novels were made into an 89-part German television series, is one of the best-known literary representatives of Cornwall. Locations for the series were scattered all over the region and in themselves provide a perfect itinerary. Land's End, near Penzance, as well as boasting imposing cliffs, golden beach and rapeseed fields, is also the home of the Cornwall and West Devon Mining World Heritage Site, where a number of historical features provide a fascinating insight into earlier industry. The picturesque town of Bodmin is further inland. To the north in Newquay there is a lively scene. With its nine unspoiled beaches and spectacular cliffs, this is a surfers' paradise. The Eden Project, the indoor jungle, is also worth seeing. It is known as the Eight Wonder of the World.

## At a glance

**Location:** part of the South West Peninsula, borders with the county of Devon in the east
**Area:** 3,546 km² / 1,370 mi²
**www.visitcornwall.com**

Lizard Point is situated on the peninsula with the Stone Age "Three Brothers of Grugith" (top). The twin octagonal towers of the Lizard Lighthouse (bottom left), dating back to 1752, also stand here.

## The Lizard

The lovely peninsula of the Lizard leads to the southernmost tip of England. We recommend a hike along the Coastal Path to Lizard Point so that you can experience this austere landscape with its sea-buffeted crags, narrow coves and small settlements up close. With its twin octagonal lighthouse towers, this marks the northern entrance to the English Channel, which has been the downfall of many ships over the years. Those interested in geology will discover that the oceanic crust was thrust to the surface here. There is nowhere else on the island where the colourful sedimentary rocks, such as serpentinite, are so well preserved.

## Penwith Heritage Coast and Land's End

The westernmost point of England is characterised by open heath and moorland, and is virtually littered with archaeological sites. Tombs from the Iron and Bronze Ages, Celtic crosses and whole villages from the pre-Christian period attest to its thousand-year old history of settlement. Atlantic waves surge unrelentingly against the massive rocks, which the Romans named Belerion (seat of storms). The tip of the peninsula is now dominated by a much-visited theme park.

## Bedruthan Steps

In a bay between Newquay and Padstow, these five enormous boulders lie on the beach in a picturesque fashion, as if they had been thrown there by supernatural powers. They inspired the imagination of travellers in early days; they ultimately concluded that they were the stepping stones of the mythological giant Bedruthan. In reality, however, they were created by the washing away of softer stone strata, including haematite. If you dare, you can climb up the staggering stairs at ebb tide and examine the boulders and surf from close up.

# BRAUNTON BURROWS - NORTH DEVON
## UNESCO Biosphere Reserve

The reserve around the dune system is under the protection of UNESCO because of its unique landscape and biological diversity. The island is known as Devon's only breeding colony for puffins.

Starting from Croyde, there is a stunning coastal road and a hiking trail leading to Saunton Sands where the five kilometre / three mile-long secluded beach in Devon spreads out - just in front of Braunton Burrows, the 141 square kilometre / 55 square mile Biosphere Reserve and the largest dune system in all of Britain. The reserve covers a large part of the coast of North Devon and also includes the estuaries of the rivers Taw and Torridge. Little paths wind through the sand-hills, salt marshes and diverse plant life. At the beginning of July, here and there a blue thyme flower flashes and in between stand yellow hawkweed and pyramidal orchids. This is where the American GIs trained for D-Day, and there are some replicas of their landing boats hidden near the car park between the dunes at the southern tip.

## At a glance

**Location:** along the north coast of Devon on the Bristol Channel
**Area:** 141 km² / 55 mi²
**Designation as UNESCO Biosphere Reserve:** 1976
**www.northdevonbiosphere.org.uk**

Turquoise-blue water and pink heather make the Exmoor National Park brighter than its gloomy legends would lead you to expect. Gorse, ferns and hawthorn trees add dots of colour to the largest continuous moor.

Gloomy stories are told in Exmoor, stories like the one about the hangman who was himself hanged. An ill-fated sheep stealer, high on a cliff, swung a rope around his neck to help lead his loot away but then ended up being strangled by it. When you travel through this plateau in the counties of Devon and Somerset, you have no trouble understanding these stories. It is a harsh world of treeless heathland, full of bogs interspersed by bottomless valleys through which the wind cuts like a thousand swords. Maybe the loneliness and the uninhabited vastness have contributed to these horror stories. But probably not the semi-wild Exmoor pony which one occasionally encounters; they are the oldest breed of ponies in the island and are more likely to make you think of girlish dreams than of spooky ghost stories.

## At a glance

**Location:** in the English counties of Devon and Somerset, bordering the Bristol Channel in the north
**Area:** 693 km² / 268 mi²
**Foundation:** 1954
**www.exmoor-nationalpark.gov.uk**

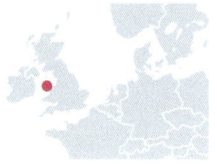

# ANGLESEY

**With its lighthouse, built in 1873, Llanddwyn Island is a magical place. Located at the far end of a pleasant beach near Newborough Warren, this narrow finger of land is an ideal picnic site.**

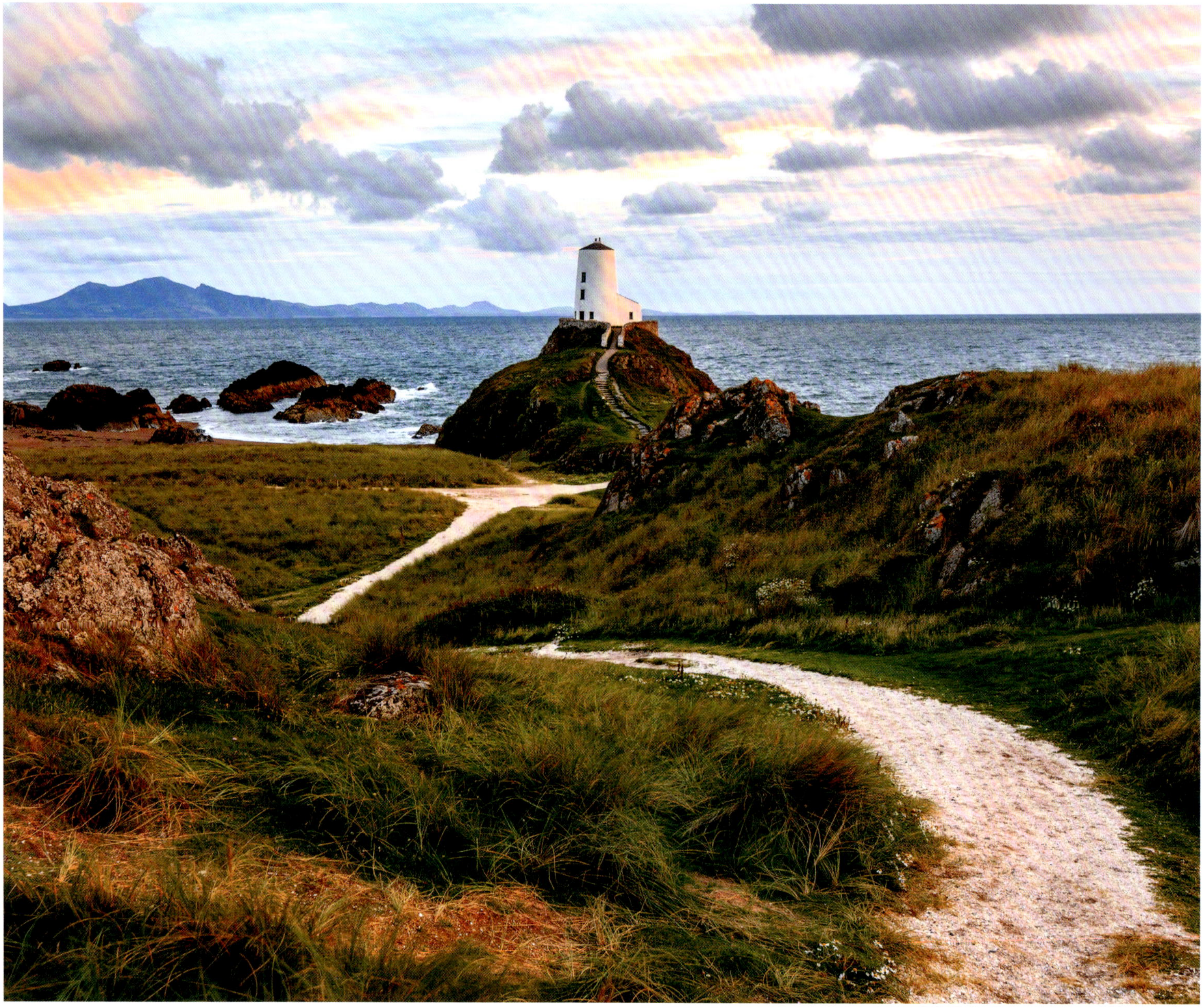

With its standing stones, ancient burial mounds, the remains of a once flourishing copper mine, a World Cultural Heritage Castle and two magnificent Victorian bridges, history is really brought to life on the wonderful island of Anglesey with its stunning coastal paths. Situated in the far northwest of Wales, it has always been refreshingly different. Here the inhabitants are self-confident enough to name a village Llanfairpwllgwyngyllgogerychwyrndrobwllllantysiliogogogoch. Off the west coast lies the tidal island of Ynys Llanddwyn, which can be reached on foot at low tide. The Tŵr Mawr lighthouse, erected in 1873, is on the island; the British film "Retreat" was filmed there in 2010. The island remains attached to the mainland apart from at the very highest tides. It provides a magnificent view of Snowdonia and the Lleyn peninsula.

## At a glance

**Location:** island off the northwest coast of Wales
**Area:** 714 km$^2$ / 276 mi$^2$

# GEOMÔN
## UNESCO Global Geopark

The lovely Geomôn UNESCO Global Geopark attracts millions of tourists with its spectacular rocky promontories and extensive sandy beaches. Archaeological sites show how humans lived here about 7,000 years ago in the Mesolithic Period. Famous local people including acclaimed artist Sir Kyffin Williams, whose great uncle was Sir Andrew Ramsay ("father of Welsh geology" in his day), supported the realisation of Geomôn from the beginning. He is considered a founding member of the park.

**The tectonic island of Anglesey is composed of more than 100 different type of rock as well as the oldest fossils in England and Wales.**

## At a glance

**Location:** on the island of Anglesey
**Area:** 720 km$^2$ / 278 mi$^2$
**Designation as UNESCO Global Geopark:** 2015

# SNOWDONIA
## National Park

The landscape of Capel Curig (large picture top) is defined by the picturesque Ogwen valley and the Llynnau Mymbyr lakes. Some of the surrounding mountains, for example Moel Siabod, rise to 900 metres / 2,953 feet.

Once there was a giant called Rhudda, and he lived on the summit of the mountain and dressed in a cape made of the hair from the beards of kings he had slain. The cape grew thicker and thicker until King Arthur came and killed the evil giant because he did not want to hand over the hair from his beard. Since then, the legend says, Rhudda rests on his mountaintop under a cairn which is called "Yr Wyddfa" in Welsh. The English name for this

is Snowdon, and not only is Snowdonia National Park in North Wales called after it, it is also its highest point. Its lakes are unfathomably blue, its mountainsides ghostly green. Often, though, all the colours are swallowed up in the mist and clouds which creep in like a silent tide and shroud the landscape. More than five metres / three feet of precipitation fall here every year; the summers are scorching hot, the winters bitterly cold and there is nowhere to hide from the biting wind.

The Llynnau Mymbyr (top) are two lakes connected by a channel in Dyffryn Mymbyr, a valley in the National Park.

## At a glance

**Location:** in the west of Wales
**Area:** 2,170 km$^2$ / 838 mi$^2$
**Foundation:** 1951
**www.visitsnowdonia.info**

# PEMBROKESHIRE COAST
## National Park

If you pass by road signs with unpronounceable names such as Fford Cilgwyn, Llwyngwair, Feidr Cefn or Gellifawr, then you know you've arrived in the wondrous world of the Pembrokeshire Coast National Park. And because these names sound like fairies and elves, in this landscape you feel like you are in a magical world of nature. This is especially due to the coast along which the Pembrokeshire Coast Path winds, one of the most stunning coastal hiking trails in Great Britain. There is not one boring inch on it since cliffs, coves and sandy beaches alternate in rapid succession. Due to the mild climate 50 different type of flowers bloom as early as January, from hyacinths to anemones. Later in the year, thousands and thousands of seabirds including oystercatchers and razorbills nest amidst this sea of colour.

## At a glance

**Location:** along the coast of Pembrokeshire in Wales
**Area:** 620 km² / 240 mi²
**Foundation:** 1952
**www.pembrokeshirecoast.wales**

The Strumble Head lighthouse on the rocky island of the same name in northern Pembrokeshire was built in 1908 to replace a light-vessel previously moored in the south of Cardigan Bay.

The Bitches, as they are called, are a well-known natural phenomenon; a tidal race or rapid which occurs in the strait between the coast and the offshore island of Ramsay. Depending on the tidal range, they appear every 12.5 hours and can be surfed with, for example, a kayak.

# BRECON BEACONS
## National Park

Gentle green hills, pretty villages and an idyllic canal - the Brecon Beacons National Park is considered a kind of Welsh cornucopia, full of scenic highlights. There is so much to discover here, from the depths of the limestone caves to the heights of Pen y Fan. Above all, though, the area is known as "waterfall country". Thus, on the Four Falls Walk, you will find impressive cascades to marvel at. The hiking trail begins at Cwm Porth car park where the

Mellte river vanishes into the largest cave entrances in Wales. A little later, you will arrive at Sgwd Clun-Gwyn, the "fall of the white meadow". From there you walk along the river to Sgwd y Pannwr which leads to Sgwd yr Eira, the "snow waterfall". Henrhyd Falls is the most famous due to Hollywood films such as the "Dark Knight Rises" (2012). It is a breathtaking 27 metres / 89 feet high but is easy to reach via a short steep path.

**The green, heather-covered mountains of the Brecon Beacons were formed over a period of nearly eight millennia.**

## At a glance

**Location:** in South Wales, about 50 kilometres / 30 miles from Cardiff
**Area:** 1,344 km² / 519 mi²
**Foundation:** 1957
**www.breconbeacons.org**

At 886 metres / 2,907 feet, Pen y Fan (large picture top) is the highest elevation in South Wales. The Tommy Jones Obelisk stands on the way to the summit; this commemorates a five-year old boy who fell here in 1900.

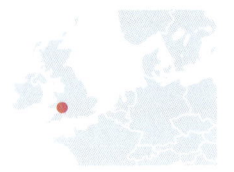

# FFOREST FAWR
## UNESCO Global Geopark

**The unusual stone row of Saith Maen is situated above Abercraf in the Tawe valley on the slopes of the 423 metre / 1,388 feet-high Cribarth. The Tawe valley (large picture) is also known as Swansea valley.**

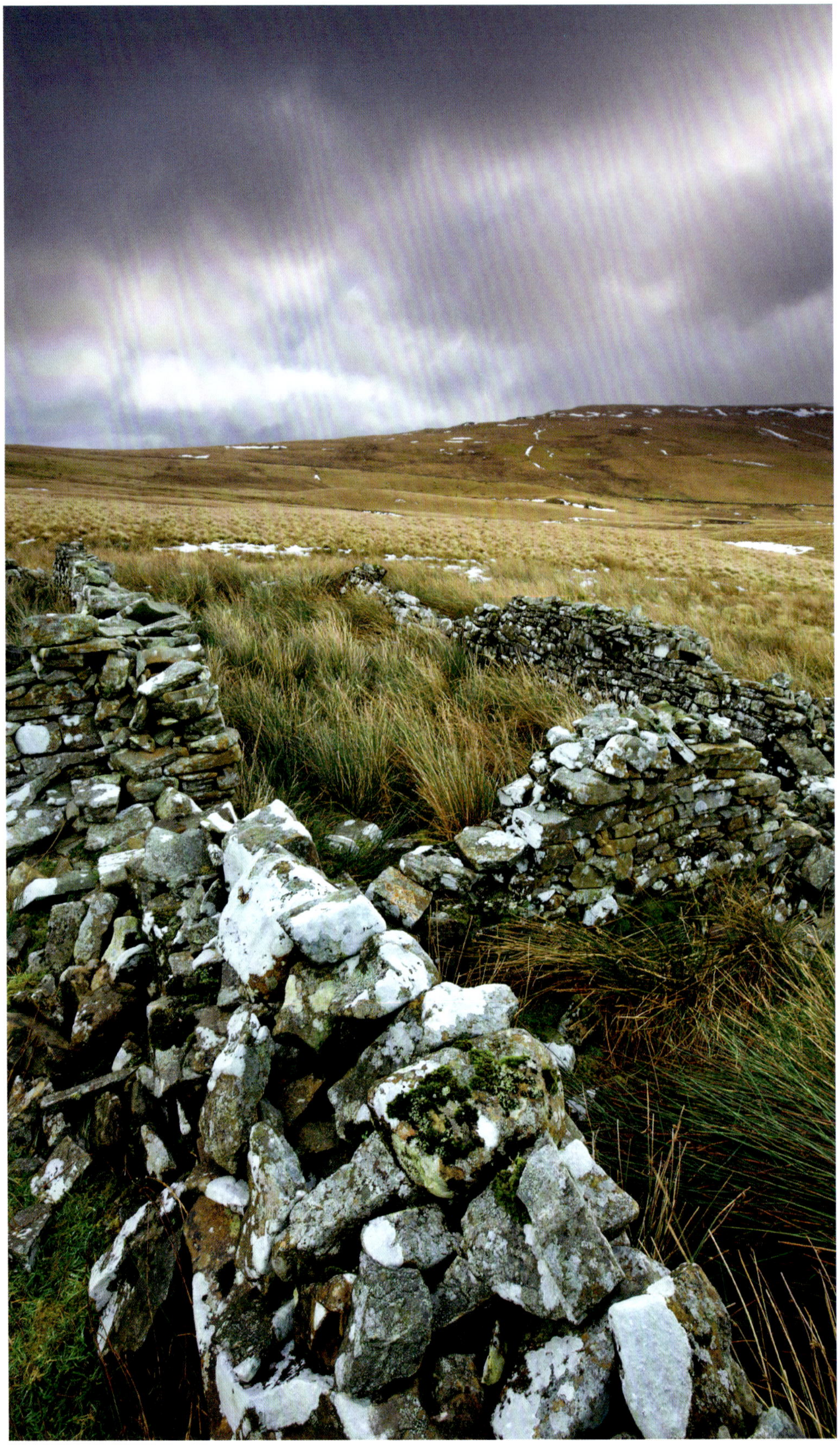

It is true that Fforest Fawr, which today is moorland, was previously wooded, but that is not why it received its name. Rather, the meaning of its name goes back to the Middle Ages when hunting grounds were referred to as forest - even though the right to hunt animals there was restricted to the local lords. Bernard de Neufmarché, Norman lord of Brecon, created this "forest" in 1100. In the

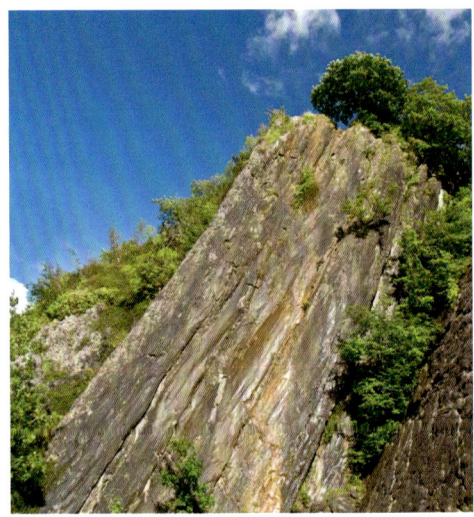

19th century, pillow mounds were built for farming rabbits in parts of the area, especially on the flanks of Cefn Cul above the Cray reservoir. Since 2005, these long low earth mounds form the core of the Fforest Fawr Geopark.

**Dinas Rock (top) is an imposing limestone cliff at the edge of the village of Pontneddfechan and is considered one of the most dangerous inland sport climbing cliffs.**

## At a glance

**Location:** extensive uplands in the county of Powys
**Area:** 763 km$^2$ / 295 mi$^2$
**Foundation:** 2005
**Designation as UNESCO Global Geopark:** 2015
**www.fforestfawrgeopark.org.uk**

In the roar of the waters: the overwhelming feeling you get when you stand beside a waterfall can be experienced up close in Mid Wales. The spates of water are somehow magical, but also soothing.

The 60 square kilometre / three square mile forest within the Dyfi biosphere, whose overall area is 840 square kilometres / 324 square miles, is situated to the north of the river Dyfi between the towns of Dolgellau and Machynlleth. Rugged peaks loom above the forested hillsides, which are dotted with atmospheric ruins and slate spoil heaps. Fast flowing mountain streams cascade down rocky valleys, edged by moss-covered oaks. The remains of several old slate mines can still be seen in the area at Abergynolwyn, Corris and Hendre Ddu. The scenic highlight of the Dyfi valley is the 747 metre / 2,450 feet-high Aran Fawddwy in Dinas Mawddwy with its stunning view over the Dyfi biosphere reserve.

**The managed wetlands in the Dyfi biosphere (top right) preserve the habitat of, among others, osprey (bottom right) which like to build their nests on storm-damaged tree tops.**

## At a glance

**Location:** in Mid Wales
**Area:** 840 km² / 324 mi²
**Foundation:** 1970
**Designation as UNESCO Biosphere Reserve:** 1977
**www.dyfibiosphere.wales**

# PICTURE CREDITS, IMPRINT

MONACO BOOKS is an imprint of Kunth Verlag GmbH & Co KG
© Kunth Verlag GmbH & Co. KG, Munich
For distribution please contact:
Monaco Books
c/o Kunth Verlag GmbH & Co. KG
St.-Cajetan-Straße 41
81669 Munich, Germany
Tel. +49.89.45 80 20-0
Fax +49.89.45 80 20-21
www.monacobooks.com
www.kunth-verlag.de
info@kunth-verlag.de

Printed in the EU

Texts: Stephanie Fischer, Katinka Holupirek, Laura Joppien, Andrea Rudolf, Iris Ottinger, Christa Pöppelmann
Translations: Travod International Ltd